EXHIBIT A

Proof that God wants you wealthy!

By

Benjamin K. Tejevo

AuthorHouse™
1663 Liberty Drive
Bloomington, IN 47403
www.authorhouse.com
Phone: 1-800-839-8640

Scriptural quotations, unless otherwise stated, are from The New International Version (NIV) Bible translation.

The quotes will be in italic and have the exact Bible verse after each quote.

Published by AuthorHouse   10/17/2012

ISBN: 978-1-4772-3042-8 (sc)
ISBN: 978-1-4772-3074-9 (e)

Cover design by: Charlene Logan Design inc.

Introduction

Hello. My name is Benjamin Keve Tejevo. I was born-again in August 2005. Since then I have been on a personal mission to achieve and experience everything God has so freely set before me.

In 2009, it was revealed to me what my calling was:
"To pull down spiritual strongholds"
So as I set out to explore what this calling actually meant, I was led by the spirit into the Business world, and then into to the financial world.
What I discovered was truly astounding but very real! One of the greatest and most powerful strongholds ever to plague mankind was Money! We are all affected by it; we all depend on it; spend and desire it. Money has power to do many things. It can make a good person bad and a bad person good. It can change our mood in an instant. Money has the ability to cause all kinds of mental changes and even encourages us to judge others based on how much of it they seemingly have. Money is power!

"How do I pull that down?" was my next question. I discovered that the answer was simpler and more achievable than the social elite had fooled us into believing. As I began to explore this new revelation with the word of God, things started to make sense, why was money so powerful? Why do people with money act so confident? Why is the world centred on money? How can I break this mentality?

Then one day the spirit said to me, He would reveal the secrets, then I would have to teach it; but first I have to live it.

So this book is my gift to you. Why not read it, or should I dare say study it and apply the principles highlighted from the word of God to your view and use of money.

You will be amazed at the results; which are actually more than money can buy. I have studied and applied these principles to my personal life and it's working for me. I sleep well at nights; I am secure both now and in my future, it hasn't been easy, it wasn't quick, but the results are everlasting.

Everything in life is hard at first until you learn how to do it.

That is lesson number one; and you are getting it in just the introduction. I pray that as you read through this book, you will apply these simple principles to your life and prove they work, and then you can teach it to others around you so they can benefit from their understanding also.

Here are just a few names of people who have applied Biblical principles to their finances and produced massive amounts of wealth for their families. Why not look them up and read up about their background and success stories for yourself.

Dale Carnegie. Says "The Bible is the ultimate blueprint for Business".

Art Williams. Founder of A.L. Williams & Associates.

Warren Buffet. The Worlds third richest man. Closest friend to **Bill Gates**. Worlds richest man.

Sam Walton. Founder of Wal-Mart. Died in 1992 as the world's richest man.

The world has discovered these principles, and are reaping the benefits. So let's apply them in our lives and see if we can produce the same results in our walk through life.

Why should I read this book?

Now that is a great question! Allow me to start things off by addressing it with these simple statistics:

Jesus spoke about money more than he did about Heaven and Earth combined.

11 out of the 39 parables Jesus told were about money, or the use of it.

1 verse of every 6 in the New Testament as a whole, deal with money.

1 in every 3 chapters on average in the gospels, Matthew, Mark, Luke and John refer to money or the use of it in one way or another.

800 Verses in the entire Bible refer to money in some way.

The Bible puts the root of all evil on the love of Money **(1Timothy 6:10)**

The Bible refers to money as a master; in other words, you can be a slave to it; rich or poor.

The first suicide to be recorded in the New Testament was to do with money:
" When Judas who betrayed him saw that Jesus was condemned, he was seized with remorse and returned the thirty pieces of silver to the chief priests and elders.
" I have sinned" he said, "for I have betrayed innocent blood" "What is that to us?" They replied; "that is your responsibility."
So Judas threw down the money in the temple and left. Then he went and hanged himself. **Matthew 27:3-5.**

The first sin recorded in the church of the New Testament was to do with money: **Acts 5: 1-10.** This is the story of how Ananias and his wife were moved by a spirit of giving, sold their land to give money to the church but lied about how much they received. The Apostles asked them, *"No one told you to sell your land and bring the money, so why would you lie to God?"*
They both dropped down dead on the spot.

The first sin in Israel which brought defeat to the whole camp is found in **Joshua 7: 20-26.** This is where Achon coveted and hid the riches of Babylon for himself. He was found out and his whole family, including everything he owned were killed and destroyed.

In all cases, none of these people ever got to spend or enjoy what they had committed the sins for. There are many more but we will go through them as the book progresses.

Why do you think the Bible, written so many years ago, put such an emphasis on money?

Money has real power. Let's be honest; it has the ability to change economies, Governments, nations, societies and in some cases even the law.

Statistics have shown that the number one cause for family and marriage break-ups in the developed world is money.

Money is the one thing we never seem to have enough of.

The number one cause of strife in any home is money; either the lack of it or the use of it.

Money can affect our mood and emotions either in a positive or negative way.

Most of us spend more time trying to make money than we do anything else; we evaluate people based on how much money they seemingly have.

Money seems to have real visible power and can convert most people, even believers, into doing all kinds of evil things. It has the ability to create a grip over all areas of our lives, most are snared by it, but thankfully Jesus said if we study His word, we will know the truth and the truth shall set us free.
John 8:31-32.

From these facts alone, you should realise by now that money itself is a powerful force which can be used for good or evil.
This is why it is so important that, as Christians, we understand money from a Biblical perspective, but at the same time learn how to control it instead of it controlling us like it does the rest of the world.

You know knowledge is power. Anybody can with the right understanding. With the right information you can be what ever you want to be, whether it is a lawyer, doctor, scientist etc.

It's all about knowing the right information.
All education does, is give you the relevant information for what ever field you have an interest in.

If you could get the understanding to break the grip money has over you, wouldn't that be good?

Now look at this: The Greek word "Doctrine" means "Teaching". It occurs a total of 30 times in the New Testament. The four Gospels refer to Jesus teaching 43 times but preaching only 19 times.
6 Verses refer to him preaching and teaching in the same verse.

This shows that Jesus spent twice as much time teaching as He did preaching, and based on His type of ministry, Jesus produced thousands of disciples who in turn went out and taught others. Basically, it is better and more beneficial for you to be taught, so you can apply these principles in order to prove them, than for someone to preach it to you.
Preaching is great, but teaching helps develop discipleship which is good for the world.

You are in control of your life. I will just be outlining a few facts according to scripture, and then you decide what you want to do with the Biblical information I will be highlighting. It will be for your own good.

Context

In this modern society in which we live, things seem to be getting more and more about the materialistic. Everything is becoming centred around money and owning material things; to the point that the church is unwisely trying to steer itself away from money and money issues. Churches seem to be avoiding dealing with this issue in case people think that we are constantly begging for money. Talking about money within the church circle makes people uncomfortable; so we tiptoe around the subject.

But answer me this, how can you help the poor if you're poor? How do you support the needy if you're needy?
I grew up in the church all my life; I've always found it strange that the church seems to be a bit squeamish when it comes to talking about money: the most essential tool in meeting people's needs.

So in this book 'Exhibit A' I will be bringing my case before you that God wants you wealthy in order to reach and convert the world into his Kingdom.
We will be looking at Biblical evidence and studying their relevancy in today's day and age as it was in the Bible days.

You are the judge and jury, you decide the verdict for yourself whether you believe it or not. The court in your mind is now in cession.

You may be seated

Contents

Layout.. 11

Remember the Lord your God.

God gets no glory out of you being poor.............. 18
The 'first fruits' principle.................................... 24
For God loves a cheerful giver............................. 26
What are you afraid of? 29
Giving can bring you closer with God................ 32
Give and it shall be given unto you...................... 34
Sow a seed.. 40
Teach it to your kids.. 44
Obedience to the command of God.................... 47
Trust in God to provide for you............................ 51
Lessons from a giver.. 55
Your Heavenly account.. 65
General offering talk.. 69

It is He who has given you the ability to produce wealth.

Man shall not live by bread alone..................... 71
Where there is no vision the people perish.... 75
The parable of the talents................................. 87
The parable of the shrewd manager.............. 123

In order to establish His covenant on the earth.

The ways versus the Acts of God..................... 147
Ruler over much... 153
The world will accept you if you just stay poor..... 157
I backslid when I saw how the ungodly prosper. 161
Why is the wealth of the ungodly being stored up? 165
Gods' storehouse... 169
Conclusion... 176

Lay out

This book will be laid out in 3 main steps, which will all be centred on the command given according to **Deuteronomy**, which reads:

Remember the Lord your God, for it is he who has given you the ability to produce wealth, in order to establish his covenant which he swore to your forefathers as it is this day.
Deuteronomy 8:18.

The reasoning behind this layout is that we need to follow exactly the pattern shown to us in scripture. Lets learn and understand how to do things Gods' way. The pattern in Deuteronomy 8:18 is; first of all learn to give back unto God a portion of what He has blessed us with already; Second, we then discover that the ability to produce more is already within us, our skill. Then finally come to the realisation that all of it is just to confirm the promise God has already made to us. It's all about Him.

Step 1: *Remember the Lord your God.*

In this step, we will be studying the importance of remembering to give unto God a portion of what He has blessed you with; heart motive in your giving, how does money affect you?
Do you give regularly and freely to a church or ministry to support God's work here on earth?

We will look at the commands associated with the tithes and offerings; always acknowledge that all you have is a tool from God to do His work while we have it.

Are we trustworthy enough to be entrusted with more? Or do we just have a selfish mentality? And therefore fall short of the requirements in the covenant.

Step 2: *For it is he who has given you the ability to produce wealth.*

This step, I believe, will be life changing! It will show that we already have the ability to produce or in some Bible translations, the power to get wealth. We already have the ability to do it. Most just don't understand this point.

It's like electricity, it has always been there from the foundations of the earth, it was always around, and the principles existed. The problem was that the people in the olden days just hadn't discovered the principles associated with using it. Once we learnt and understood the laws associated with controlling electricity, people put them into operation, and we are so blessed today because we know how to use it.

God didn't just make electricity recently, He had already set down the laws from the beginning; it just took thousands of years to discover these principles.

So even today, there are certain things we haven't yet discovered that in just a few years' time, when the next generation discover it, they too will look back at us and wonder how we ever managed without what ever it is. And so it was with gravity, TV, mobile technology and so on.

Understand that the command and principles for all things that sustain life have already been given from the creation of the planet in the first few days. God has already done all he needed to do, it is just up to us humans, his most precious creation to discover and put into practice the principles associated with making something work.

So in this step, we are already blessed because the Bible tells us that God has already given us the ability to produce wealth.

All we need to do is understand and put the principles in this section into practice in regards to handling money and our own unique talents / skill.

Then one day, we too will discover wealth for ourselves.

Now that's definitely worth reading on for.

I live by certain rules which I always try to apply in any situation I come across. These rules aid me in my decision making and most importantly, in understanding most things. Here's one I would like you to learn and apply to everything and every area of your life.

Never the how, always the why!

This rule will help you view all things from a self motivating and empowering perspective. You will no longer be limited by the worries of **How** can I do something? But you will look forward to the end result of **Why** I should do something.

I will be applying this rule in step three as we try to understand why God says He has given us the ability to produce. Don't worry yet about how you are going to produce wealth; that might take up all your time, and you will begin by thinking this book is a get-rich-quick scheme. Then if you read it you expect to be wealthy in 5 days. If that doesn't happen, you give up and just go back to doing life as you always have; then you say that was a waste of time.

So let's look at why God has given us this ability to produce wealth.

Step 3: *In order to establish His covenant, which He swore to your forefathers, as it is this day.*

Now this is my favourite step. It basically states that God wants us wealthy; and the purpose of it is to establish or fulfil His covenant which He swore to our forefathers. So you could even put it this way: God has sworn that you should be wealthy.

A lot of people read this portion of scripture but don't truly dig deep enough to understand the true meaning. So before we go on, we need to fully understand this portion; because the entire book is based upon this covenant God himself has sworn to us.

You will not benefit from the principles in this book unless you understand this covenant fully, so let me explain it.

First of all, wherever you read in the Bible "as it is this day" it simply refers to the day in the Bible time, and now, today. So it transfers from the Bible days, to this present day and age. It is a promise that keeps on going from generation to generation to all the children of God. When you become born-again you automatically enter into that promise.

But what is the covenant? The answer is found in a number of scriptures in the Old Testament, but let's use the simplest interpretation explained in the book of Jeremiah.

Then I will fulfil the oath I swore to your forefathers, to bring them into a land flowing with milk and honey.
Jeremiah 11:15.

The covenant is to bring His beloved (which is us), into a land flowing with milk and honey. Now if this is clear enough, your next question should be, "how can you have a land flowing milk and honey?" It doesn't make sense; nature cannot be sustained with milk and honey! You are correct, that is not possible. So let's dig deeper to find the true meaning of this covenant.
Milk, is something you don't have to work for, all you need to do is go and get it. The entire production process has already been carried out by the cows. You make the decision when you want some to just go and grab it.
It's already ready.

Honey, is another thing you don't have to work for. The entire production process has also already been done for you by the bees.

The collecting of the pollen from different flowers, the manufacturing process all the way down to the final product, has been taken care of.

Its already ready, you just have to get up, go and receive it.

Now understand this, God made the cows and the bees in the first place who in turn produces the milk and honey, which are Gods' provision. So the real meaning of this covenant in **Deuteronomy 8:18**, is that God wants you wealthy in order to bring you into a land or time or even a point in your life flowing with His provision.

That is awesome, all God really wants to do is provide for you; He wants to take care of you. You really need to understand this before we can move on; God is a loving father who wants nothing but the best for His children.

No matter how the intellectuals try to analyse this book, even if the enemy brings confusion or doubt into your head as you study these principles in your life, bring them back to this point that according to this passage **Deuteronomy 8:18**, you cannot experience this covenant without wealth, you cannot experience Gods' provision without wealth.

Gods' provision is wealth. The ability to help and reach a hungry world is going to be through wealth.

Please allow me to make a point here; this wealth is not to fulfil your own worldly desires. It is not to serve your own agenda; you won't be receiving it so that you become bigheaded and start comparing yourself with others and looking down on people.
It will not be yours to please you but to please God as you enhance His Kingdom.

God delights in the prosperity of his servants.
Psalm 35:27 :

This wealth is to benefit the Kingdom of God. You are to use it, but if you abuse it you will lose it.
This book is basically a tool, to prepare you for what is your promise according to the immutable and unchangeable word of God.
When you align yourself with Gods' agenda and commands, according to His principles, you will then be able to receive this wealth, not for any selfish gain. The purpose of wealth is to establish Gods' covenant here on earth in this present day.

Remember the Lord your God.

God gets no glory out of you being poor.
Acts 10: 1-4

To get things kicked off, I would like us to begin with the end result. This way, if you don't like or agree with what you are reading, you can stop reading straight away and save yourself time. Give this book to someone else who you believe would benefit from it more than you. It is my will that as you read this book you come to the understanding that, if God created us all for His pleasure, He can only be pleased and glorified through our lives being lived according to His purpose. He has not created a single failure! The world has! So it is Gods' will that we return to our former glory of what He had intended all along, His inheritance.
I know this might sound a bit strong and kind of rude, but please understand this; my intentions are pure, my words are spoken out of love, and everything I do is for the benefit of the Kingdom of Heaven.

Let's begin by studying the life of a seemingly outsider, someone who was outside of Gods' chosen people, yet living as God intended for His people.

His is a story of a man whose character is exactly what God is looking for in all believers. Cornelius wasn't a Christian but he had all the personality of a true God-fearing believer.

Let us understand one thing first of all, God gets no glory out of you being poor; can't pay your bills, can't afford healthy food, malnourished, unable to even get yourself to church. God gets no glory out of you proclaiming to be a Christian, yet when food prices go up, you start to doubt and begin moaning about it like the rest of the world; when petrol prices increase, we start to panic like the unbelievers.

Those are bad advertisements for the Kingdom of Heaven. What do we have to offer if we are just as scared and fragile as the rest of the world? If there is no visible difference between believers and unbelievers, then what is the point?

We are supposed to be the salt and light of the earth:

You are the salt of the earth. But if the salt loses its saltiness, how can it be made salty again? It is no longer good for anything, except to be thrown out and trampled by men. You are the light of the world. A city on a hill cannot be hidden. Neither do people light a lamp and put it under a bowl. Instead they put it on its stand, and it gives light to everyone in the house. In the same way, let your light shine before men, that they may see your good deeds and praise your father in heaven.
Matthew 5:13-14.

We are meant to be more than conquerors:

No, in all these things we are more than conquerors through him who loved us.
Romans 8:37

We are supposed to be the head and not the tail:

The Lord will make you the head, not the tail. If you pay attention to the commands of the Lord your God that I give you this day and carefully follow them, you will always be at the top, not the bottom.
Deuteronomy 28:13.

We have unintentionally allowed ourselves to become trapped by an economic system, which has so snared us that we are advertising Christianity as "I'm poor, but at least I'm going to heaven and you rich people aren't!"
That is a completely wrong attitude to have. We are living so far beneath our privileges as children of God.

This man named Cornelius was an unbeliever, but living the life which God had intended for all his children; so this caused God to send an angel to tell him how to be accepted into the Kingdom; basically, 'I need you in my camp'.

What he was exhibiting in his character is exactly what Christians are supposed to become; God-fearing, generous, able to give to those in need at any time, caring, highly regarded in the community. In a position of authority, he had people under his command. Trustworthy, he was in charge of a regiment which meant he could be trusted to make life-changing decisions.

This is what God wants for his children, and since Cornelius wasn't part of the Israelites, an angel was sent to tell him that everything he has been doing so far has been pleasing to God. He was accepted into the Kingdom.

At Caesarea there was a man named Cornelius, a centurion in what was known as the Italian regiment. He and all his family were devout and God-fearing; he gave generously to those in need and prayed to God regularly. One day about three in the afternoon he had a vision. He distinctly saw an angel of God, who came to him and said, "Cornelius!" Cornelius stared at him in fear. "What is it, Lord?" he asked. The angel answered, "Your prayers and gifts to the poor have come up as a memorial offering before God.
Acts 10: 1-4.

Let me just give you the background here, as this entire book is going to be based around **Deuteronomy 8:18**, that is at the point when the Israelites (Gods' chosen people) had entered and settled into the promised land; they had been fed, all their dreams had finally come true, they were full, in need of nothing, life was good. So in that scripture, God was revealing to them, and us in today's present day, that having all your dreams come true, safety and security, enough food and so on, is not the end goal. They had everything, but did not yet have the power to produce.
So first of all, you need to get this in your mind; it is not about money! It is about having the power to do! Money and your use of it is the training ground.

If this is Gods' desire for every believer, then why aren't we all experiencing this? Well that's simple; we do not obey Gods' command! We do not trust and rely on His word! The one thing God desires from us is our obedience; do what I say! Have faith! Do not be afraid! Do not worry! I am your God.

Here's a simple command spoken to all Bible believers:

If you are willing and obedient, you will eat the best from the land.
Isaiah 1:19.

How simple is that? But most have become so money orientated in our thinking that we have pierced ourselves with this worldly 'I want, I want' attitude which is limiting our ability to becoming a blessing to others. Every true honest believer will tell you that they have a burden for the Kingdom of God; they have ideas of how to help others, be it missionary work, opening a shelter for the needy, building a church, helping children in need, forming an organisation to re-habilitate young offenders and so on.

These are all great ideas which would greatly demonstrate and extend the love of God to those in desperate need of a saviour.

But how can we do it if we've got work in the morning? How can we reach out to those people, when we are just about keeping up with our monthly commitments? And it feels like the government is just trying to squeeze the life out of us!

You see, there is no lack of the desire to want to do! There is no lack of good motivations and intentions!

But that's not good enough; that's not going to cut it. What we have, is the lack of the ability to do. What we lack is the power to achieve these things! So as long as the enemy can keep us poor in our thinking, we will never reach our full potential.

I would recommend that you study the entire story of Cornelius when you can, you will find that he had the ability to help the needy, the power to influence others, so God sent the Holy Spirit to empower them all when they heard the gospel.

This book is not a get rich quick scheme, but if you apply yourself to the principles highlighted in it, you will not only have wealth, you will have the power and the ability to produce wealth.

Why not study also the entire chapter of Deuteronomy twenty eight, and see how much God rewards obedience, and curses disobedience.

Remember the Lord your God

The 'first fruits' principle
Proverbs 3:9-10

The most important tithe in the Bible is known as
the first fruits. This is ten percent of your income,
however it comes. But why is the first so
important?

When we study the creation of the world in Genesis,
we see that God did not create everything in the
first days; He only created the first of everything,
and then gave it the command and ability to
reproduce after its own kind. Everything was
created, and within itself, it was then given the
ability to re-create. Ever since the creation of the
world, everything has been in perfect harmony
according to that command.

So if you would align yourself up with this
command of bringing ten percent of your
household income into the house of God, this
principle will have to work for you.

*Honour the Lord with your wealth, with the first
fruits of all your crops; then your barns will be
filled to overflowing, and your vats will brim over
with new wine.*
Proverbs 3: 9-10.

From this, we are able to tell that it is detrimental
to your prosperity, to take your tithes anywhere
else.

If you want to be obedient to the word of God, give Him the first and let him command it to reproduce after its own kind. He is the God of the first; he can multiply one into overflowing, through his word.

When you bring your first fruits to God, you are actually acknowledging that he is first in your life; you are giving him, and the work of the ministry, priority over everything else. In times of economic hardships, if you would continue to put God first, you are actually showing where your trust and hope is. God only needs the first in order to sustain. During creation only the first was created, and it has been re-creating ever since.

When you bring your tithe despite your financial situation, you are building up your faith in God, and basically saying, "Lord, I know that you can put this to better use than I ever could." You are investing in your future, as you are building up your faith in God's ability to provide for you, despite what is going on in the world all around you.

So be wise in what you give priority to! Prove God to be true in this principle and make it work for you.

For God loves a cheerful giver.
2 Corinthians 9:7

When we study in Genesis the creation of the world, we see very clearly that, as God gets to the point of creating man, he says; "let us make man in our image." The word image means; likeness, portrayal, representation, impression, public image, persona, impression and 'similar to in characteristics!
So, God wanted to show off his character when he created us. Now consider this passage:

Each man should give what he has decided in his heart to give, not reluctantly or under compulsion, for God loves a cheerful giver.
2 Corinthians 9:7.

This request that we should give cheerfully, is a sign of God's heart, his character as a giver. As we look through scripture, we see God as a loving father, who delights in taking care of us through giving. So how does this apply to us? It simply reveals that God loves it when his character begins to shine through us into the world. It also shows that God looks at our attitude and motive behind giving, not how much or how little we give.
He loves a cheerful giver, so when you give to a church or ministry, don't kiss your money good bye when the offering basket comes round, that's the wrong attitude.

I have never been to a supermarket, and seen someone at the counter, when its time to pay, pull out their money, kiss it and say, "Goodbye money, I could have really used you." Nobody does that when they are paying for something. Could it be because they can see the immediate value of what they just spent that money on?

Well if that's the case, let me just reveal to you what happens to your money when you give it to a local church or ministry; The money is used in various ways, to fund the building, keep the lights and the heating on, in some cases feed the hungry and carry out missionary work, support the minister in preaching the good news of Jesus Christ. When you give you are basically funding God's work here on earth.

With the consistent tithes and offerings we give to the church, lives are being changed for the better. Let me share this quick story with you, this should help put things into perspective. Last year, 2010, in our church, I came across a young teenage girl who had begun self harming. Her mother found out. Not really knowing what to do in such a difficult situation, said to her daughter, "You better start going to that church with your dad". So the daughter started coming to the church. I asked her why such a beautiful, well educated, talented young girl would do that. She said, "I felt worthless, life had nothing to offer me, and I had nothing I was doing really."

Devastating story, could have turned out a lot worse, but now she has been coming to the church, her life has changed completely, she feels great about herself, feels and looks more confident, just enjoying everyday life as it comes.

Now thanks to our constant support of the church through our offerings, the church doors stayed open, the gospel was preached to her and she feels like she has something to live for. She sings with the worship team, goes out on evangelical missions to talk to others, she has more to offer life now than ever before. She is doing great. A life saved through the word. Now that's value for money however you look at it.

Giving to a church or ministry which teaches the unconditional love of God is the best use of your money. So when you give, essentially you could be saving the life of others; you're changing the world for the better. So give cheerfully, you're doing mankind a great service, that's a good use of some of your money.

This is why God loves a cheerful giver.

What are you afraid of?

We are looking at applying Biblical principles to
your use or the way you think about money. We
have seen that there is no lack of the desire to want
to help others. But how can we help if we need
help? There are certain results you get when you
put into practice certain laws. Biblical principles
mean, doing things God's way; which is not selfish
or for personal gain, but for the benefit of His
Kingdom. For God looks at the heart; so you might
try to apply some of these principles just hoping to
gain things for your self, but it won't work for you!
You have to operate according to all requirements
of the principle in order for it to produce the results
it was intended. A selfish person for example, will
in no way be able to make these principles work for
them.

*One man gives freely, yet gains even more;
another withholds unduly, but comes to poverty. A
generous man will prosper; he who refreshes
others will himself be refreshed.*
Proverbs 11: 24-25.

This principle is used to create an unselfish nature
in you; it encourages you to think of others, if you
can learn to give freely, and begin to allow God to
bless others through you, He will get more to you.

Now, you might say "that doesn't make sense! How can you give and still have more?"

Well, in Gods Kingdom that's how it works. There are many passages in scripture that prove this, so let us study the most well known incident right now.

When Jesus looked up and saw a great crowd coming towards him, he said to Philip, "Where shall we buy bread for these people to eat?" He asked this only to test him, for he already had in mind what he was going to do. Philip answered him, "Eight months wages would not buy enough bread for each one to have a bite!" Another of his disciples, Andrew, Simon Peter's brother, spoke up, "Here is a boy with five small barley loaves and two small fish, but how far will they go among so many?" Jesus said, "Make the people sit down." There was plenty of grass in that place, and the men sat down, about five thousand of them. Jesus then took the loaves, gave thanks, and distributed to those who were seated as much as they wanted. He did the same with the fish. When they had all had enough to eat, he said to his disciples, "Gather the pieces that are left over. Let nothing be wasted." So they gathered them and filled twelve baskets with the pieces of the five barley loaves left over by those who had eaten.
John 6:5-13.

Wow, what an awesome miracle; this is basically a blueprint for the church; share the Gospel to the world, then meet their needs!

The people were hungry, there were five thousand people but only one boy dared to offer his little bit of food.

In his eyes he was probably thinking, "This isn't enough, it's not much. If I offer it, it won't help a bit." Maybe others had food and they thought like that as well, so they didn't speak up or offer it. But this is a trick from the enemy to keep you from trusting God with the little you have. This boy just offered it without hesitation or thought of how it will be used; he just gave! Now through his giving, a mighty miracle was performed right in front of his eyes.

So you might be saying, "But God, what I have is not much for me and my family, if I give this little bit of nothing, I won't have any for myself."
But see what happens when we offer it to Jesus to use. He blesses it, and then uses it to meet the needs of the people till they want no more. So what are you afraid of? Are you allowing the enemy to blind you? Are you being deceived into thinking that you don't have much to give? Are you being limited by your own needs being met first, before you would think of others?

I have studied this passage many times, and it does not say anywhere that because this boy gave the only food he had, he starved to death! In fact, the scripture states that, not only was it used to feed five thousand people, but there were twelve basketfuls left over. In other words, even the boy that gave also ate till he could eat no more. So don't worry about the little you have, as long as you can use it according to the word of God, it shall be returned back unto you, pressed down, shaken together, and running over (*Luke 6:38*).

Giving can bring you into a closer relationship with God!

The work that some churches do in today's day and age is absolutely phenomenal: reaching the poor; the hungry; widows; orphans; drug addicts; alcoholics, the broken people of the world. By being associated with the work of God for so long, I have noticed that all these things are good, and great things to be involved in. People give freely to a church or ministry, then that money is used to carry out those great missions.

So, let's say that if the money is given freely, and is being used to do these things, what is happening to those who are actually doing the giving?

Well, as I was looking to find the answer, I noticed that' yes, those are great exploits; but the real work that was going on within the church, is the word of God being taught. And it was the word of God that was actually empowering and motivating people to want to carry out those missions; to spread the love of God to a hurting world.

A survey that was carried out on various churches, found that, on average in any one church, only about twenty percent of the members are consistent givers and tithers. These twenty percent actually do eighty percent of the work in the church, and always give freely.

The same survey showed that on average, only about twenty percent of the members of a church have had a real encounter with the Holy Spirit. These are the people who are reliable; others in the church can and do call upon them for support and guidance.

These people have a deep and meaningful relationship with Christ. And in ten to twenty years' time, they will still be Christians, following and serving God wholeheartedly.

Despite their past, they are better people, righteous, and on the right path. Why not test this out for yourself? If you're in a church, if there is someone you know to be very spiritual, close to God, mature in the word, just ask them if they tithe; ask if they give freely at every opportunity. Why not ask if God has ever let them down yet?

From this, I learned that maybe it is possible that our giving can actually bring you closer, and into a deeper relationship with God. The proof is already out there, clear to see. It is your obedience to God's command that brings you closer to Him. You see, when the Bible says 'give and it shall be given unto you', the blessing is not in the command. It is your obedience to the command that entitles you to the blessings.

Perhaps you who still don't understand what this book is proving. You think, what I'm outlining doesn't make sense. You think that all us church folk want is for you to give away all your money, and be poor, and then God will love you and let you into heaven. You are missing the point!

God works on you from the inside out; He draws you closer to Him, and makes your life better. You don't need to be poor!

A good man leaves an inheritance for his children's children **Proverbs 13:22.**

Give and it shall be given unto you (Part 1)
Luke 6:38.

This portion of scripture is very well known and is used in churches world wide to encourage or motivate people to give freely to the work of God.
Now there is nothing wrong with that. It is a perfect and simple scripture in regards to giving to support a ministry. It is the word of God, it's a good motivator. It's like a money-back guarantee. It's true, and it works. I myself have proved this principle many times over.

So that's all well and good, we should continue to use this, but it is elementary, it is a continuing or replenishing principle. It never runs out, when you give you get replenished so you can give again. This is a principle which is used to draw you in, to bring you into a place of trusting and believing the word of God to be true, it's reliable.

Give and it shall be given unto you. A good measure, pressed down, shaken together and running over, shall men give into your bosom. For with the same measure that you meet withal, it shall be measured unto you again.
Luke 6:38.

The only issue with this is that it is most times misunderstood. We can become so desperate in our financial situation that we just give our money away because we are in need. We want more giving back to us.

As we read on, we will learn that it is not about giving because we need it returned back to us; it's not about giving out of our need but out of our abundance. If you really want to grow up in the things of God, you have to move on from that elementary thinking, where this principle stops working.

Now when this happens, if you're the type of person who then thinks "this isn't working anymore" so you get offended and leave a church or you stop giving. You should ask yourself this question, what was your motivation behind your giving in the first place?
If it was just to have it giving back to you, then why don't you just keep your money? Stop wasting time, keep your money and pay your bills, cut out the middle man.

But if your real motivation is to truly support a church in keeping the gospel of the Kingdom going so that others can hear the good news and be saved, then that is a good reason to keep giving, that type of offering is acceptable and pleasing to God.
Children of God, we need to understand that things in God move from level to level. If your real motivation is that you are giving out of obedience to God's command, then you will be ready for the next level of prosperity.

So as God moves you up a level, this principle at the elementary stage stops working, if you lose your motivation or faith, you will only be doing yourself more harm than good because you will be missing out on what God is getting ready to do in your life.

It's like when you are training a child. To begin with, you give them little treats or rewards to motivate them to keep trying and stay interested. But after a while you stop rewarding them because it should have now become a part of their character, and they move on to bigger and better things, more responsibility as it were.

If my son who is 3 years old now, after training him to use the toilet on his own, comes up to me when his is 17 and says "Dad I used the toilet by myself can I have a cookie?" I would think something was wrong with him.
He is either not mentally capable of growing up or his motivation in learning to use the toilet by himself was just so he could get a cookie.
But when his character is built up, he can handle more responsibility, he receives more from me; and so it is with the things of God, we need to move on and graduate to bigger blessings and greater rewards for our obedience to His word.

So when you give to a person, Church or Ministry, you need to look at your motivation for doing so. If it is out of love or compassion or a command from God, then it doesn't matter how big or small your gift is, it will be pleasing in the sight of God.

So give freely and cheerfully, give with thanksgiving that you have more than enough to spare, you can actually give and still be satisfied with what you have left.

Give out of abundance, not out of need.

Give and it shall be given unto you (Part 2)
Luke 6:38.

As we saw in part 1, the motivation behind your giving is more important than what you actually give. More importantly, if your giving is motivated by God's command, and you are developing a character of giving or generosity, you then move up a level of trusting and relying on God's ability to take care and provide for you. You then begin to grow up in Christ. You are becoming a soldier for the Kingdom where you don't expect a cookie every time you say 'yes sir!'

You are becoming reliable, steadfast, committed and obedient to God's order; you are being found faithful with the little you were given. Now this is when God can begin to release more because you have proved that your motivation is not just about receiving, but becoming a blessing to others. Blessings can actually flow through you.

A lot of the time Christians, or the modern church, approaches God with such a pleading, begging mentality. Oh God I'm so poor please help me, God if you help me pay my bills this month I promise to start giving my tithes and offerings. Oh God if you do this for me I will do that for you. We are negotiating with God from a weak, worn out, tired, stressed, exhausted beggar's perspective, oh God help us. This mentality is wrong! How can a child of a King be poor?

It is only possible if they haven't truly realised who they really are, what is their inheritance, what's rightfully theirs. We need to know and believe who we are.

What I love about this passage we are using **(Luke 6:38)**, is it actually shows you where God is encouraging us to grow up to. It says *"shall men give into your bosoms"* (in the Bible, in certain contexts when you come across men, it is referring to men and women in general). So look at this *"shall men give into your bosoms",* you should ask yourself this question! Who are those men?

Well the answer is this; we are supposed to be those men! God wants us to grow up and move from a wanting needy state, into a state of generosity. We are supposed to graduate from the 'give and it shall be given unto you' state to a level of such abundance where you are releasing freely not just to a church but also to fellow Christians who are in need.

We should no longer have the character of begging, gimme, gimme, gimme, but we should now have the character of giving, releasing God's blessings to wherever it is needed.

You see, from this scripture alone you will learn that God wants to make you a channel through whom he can reach a hurting, hungry and needy world. If you have a selfish 'what can I get out of this religion', 'all about me' mentality then God can't get his blessing through you. He will just wait till you mature or until a more suitable channel becomes available.

But it will always go through the stages of: first you need, then you don't need, and then you provide. We are supposed to be the light of the world, the salt of the earth. So if you are easily shaken and panicky about petrol prices rising, food prices, recessions, and general cost of living going up; if your prosperity and level of giving is determined by worldly events, then I'm sorry but your trust is not completely in God. You haven't yet proved him to be able to take care of you through anything.

It's a hurting world out there, how can we reach them if we are just as hurt as they are? If we're just as worried, scared and hungry as they are, it's not possible. If the world is complaining about the cost of living in the work places, the bars and pubs, then people run to church for peace and we are complaining about the same things, then what makes us any different? What can we actually offer them?

They need a place of escape and it should be the church, this is God's intention. So today I challenge you to take a step of faith and commit to becoming a channel through which God's blessing can flow. It begins with your giving, however big or small; God will be looking at your heart motivation.

So just do it, trust in God, and give him the opportunity to surprise you.

Sow a seed
2 Corinthians 9:6

In the church realm, money is referred to as a seed. We hear it a lot, sow a seed into a ministry, sow into the life of others and so on.
This is correct because it's a Biblical principle of sowing and reaping.

Remember this: who ever sows sparingly will also reap sparingly, and whoever sows generously will also reap generously.
2 Corinthian 9:6

This portion is talking about sowing and reaping. It is addressing your money and its use; likening your money to a seed.
The Bible is calling money a seed. The reason it uses a natural analogy to describe money, is because you cannot cheat nature. The rules that govern nature are set! No matter where you go in the world, the rules remain the same. It still applies that if you plant a seed, it will grow and produce more. The principles for where you plant that seed are consistent because God gave the first command of reproduction after its own kind! This order is set and cannot be broken.
So when money is viewed from this perspective, it then has to operate according to the principles of multiplying or reproducing after its own kind.

The word multiply means: "to increase in number or quantity, increase by reproducing". The word reproduce in Biblical terms is "after its own kind" so in other words, you can make your money grow and reproduce more based on where you plant it.

Have you ever noticed that if most of your money goes on bills it continues to produce more money for bills? And you wonder "how come I never seem to have enough left over for myself?" You may even get a pay rise each year but yet it doesn't seem to make a difference. Do you feel like that? Or how about this, you begin by borrowing, either a loan or credit card and start paying into what you borrowed, but it doesn't go down. It begins to reproduce after its own kind, so one card reproduces another, then another, then they reproduce a loan, then store cards; You then consolidate into a bigger loan and you continue in this cycle and wonder what is going on in this house? It only started with one loan, or card.

For many people, it becomes too late and we hear about debt problems all the time. We begin thinking "well everyone else is in debt and just as miserable as me so it must be ok, it's just the norm". That is a lie and a deception from the world. That's what they want you to think. It's not ok! You don't have to remain in that state, you are allowing the enemy to use God's principle of reproducing after its own kind in a negative way to keep you enslaved and limited by debt.

So when it comes, or you get the opportunity to re-plant or sow into a fertile ground, like the Kingdom of God through tithes and offerings to the Church, you are being fooled into believing "I need to pay my bills first. When I clear all my debts I will start giving to support God's work here on earth."
Then you go back into the cycle of reproducing negative equity.

The reproduce after its own kind principle has already been set. If most of your money goes into paying bills and debts, it will produce more bills and debts after its own kind.
You know, a business man probably has more debt than you do. An organisation relies heavily on government or bank funded loans, but they don't sit down and complain, No! They plant the money where it reproduces, then use the reproduced funds to service the debts. They don't use all their profits to pay back their loans; it is used to make more money. There is a saying "money follows money". This is true! It is according to this passage:

For everyone who has will be given more, and he will have an abundance. Who ever does not have, even what he has will be taken from him.
Matthew 25:29.

Now if you understand this principle of money reproducing where it is sown, you can then see things from Gods perspective. It is his desire according to **Deuteronomy 8:18** that we are wealthy in order to establish His covenant. In other words, He wants to give us more, but if we aren't wise with where to plant it effectively for the good of the Kingdom, it can overwhelm us.

As long as you still have that mentality of 'me me me', ' I have got to service my bills, pay off my debts and so on', God will just continue to wait until you are ready.

So don't get annoyed if you find yourself continuing to beg and ask God for more money, a pay rise, a better job and so on. This will continue while you are not realising where you plant the majority of your money and how it is being reproduced.

This is why you haven't been increased yet! Because if He does give you more, and you continue giving priority to your debts and bills, the money will just keep reproducing as it always has been; negatively. But today you can change, prove this principle in a positive way. Start by sowing a little into God's work. You see God is aware that we are human, so He has no problem that we spend mass amounts on our pleasures, cars, TVs and gadgets. He knows we desire these things, so He gives us a get out of jail clause, He commands that you bring ten percent of your first fruits, your income into His house.

He is basically saying "give me priority, let me be the first thought for your money, then I can increase you as you sow into my Kingdom".

Teach it to your kids
Malachi 3:10

I will be using this scripture later on in this book, but for now, I want to focus in on the second part of it;

"Bring the whole tithe into the storehouse, that there may be food in my house. Test me in this" says the Lord Almighty, "and see if I will not throw open the floodgates of Heaven and pour out so much blessing that you will not have enough room for it."
Malachi 3:10

This encourages us to test God. This here is a very strong statement, because God is basically saying, "If you want to find out who I am, and what I can do for you, then do this" All we have to do to receive, is obey. A lot of us read this and think, "I'm too old; have too great a financial burden, too much responsibility to apply these principles; I'm in too much debt to start giving some of my income away; my job doesn't pay enough." And so on and so forth.

One day as I was preparing to teach on this point in our church. God began to speak to me about those who think in this way. He said we are limiting our potential and missing out on what he has laid up for us. He said, this is such a human mentality that we wait till things are hard before we do anything different.

We wait till we're hooked on smoking before we start trying to quit;
We wait till we're alcoholics before we start trying to give up and seek help; wait till we're drug addicts before we go into re-hab;
We wait till we're obese, and then start dieting;
Wait until we are in financial meltdown and heavily in debt before we start trying to get help and cutting back on our spending.
The problem is, it takes a long while to get into those situations but yet we want to get out of it overnight! We are not willing to put in as much effort to get out as we did to get in.

There are no quick fixes to undo what took you years to do! So let's just be real about that, it is going to take effort.
So if you are under that illusion that you are too far gone to start applying the principles highlighted in this book, and to test God on his word, then you should at least teach them to your children. If you don't have any, teach your neighbours' kids, your friends' kids. Because basically, the excuses you have are not good enough. Teach these principles to the children before they have the same excuses you are trying to use. Let's get the next generation of Christians living in God's infinite abundance.

I have heard many stories of people waiting till it was seemingly too late; waiting till their last penny before calling on the name of Jesus and him helping them. I have come across many people at rock bottom, applying these Biblical principles and gaining massive success through them.

The most impressive example I have come across to date, was the holiday destination in which my family and I went in Egypt, Sham-El Sheik.

I met the owner of the royal Savoy and Soho square complex. He told us, (if I remember the story well), he was bankrupt; had nothing left, Then he decided to try things God's way and started going to a church from morning till night.

To cut a long story short, one day he said to God, "if you just help me through this situation, I will always give to support your church." God then replied to him saying, "I just want ten percent of your income." So he began to give ten percent of what he had left. He was bankrupt, God taught him about tithing; nine years later we are staying at the best resort I have ever been to; second best holiday of my life, (my honeymoon being the best obviously). He is now a multi, multi millionaire; he has a massive development, many hotels in Egypt and so on, and till today he still tithes even more than when he began. God honoured him as much as he honoured God, and he gives all the thanks and glory to God.

So if you trust and obey God, support his ministry here on earth according to his word "test me in this and I will throw open the floodgates of heaven."
You will have an abundance that you have to share with others if you do not give up.

Obedience to the command of God.
Malachi 3:8-10

I remember when the spirit began to speak this to me; I was a bit worried about teaching it in our church. It's a little bit edgy, it's on the borderline between offending and liberating, which way will it rub you? Can people handle this?
This is a real telling off, how would people respond to it?
Then the following day, after studying and preparing the talk, the spirit spoke to me again and said, " it is time my people grow up, start obeying my command no matter how it sounds, just do it, it's for their own good." Man I was fired up after that. It was a reassurance that we need to hear this, I will tell it to anyone who will listen.

So, do you want to grow up? Are you willing to mature in the things of God? Or are you just happy circulating and remaining in the state you are in?
It's up to you, but for those who are willing to become mature Christians please read on.

"Will a man rob God? Yet you rob me. "But you ask, "How do we rob you?" "In tithes and offerings. You are under a curse-the whole nation of you- because you are robbing me. Bring the whole tithe into the storehouse, that there may be food in my house. Test me in this," says the Lord Almighty, "and see if I will not throw open the floodgates of heaven and pour out so much blessing that you will not have enough room for it."
Malachi 3:8-10.

This scripture says that we are actually robbing God by withholding our tithes and offerings. (In the next chapter, I will show how we are doing this.)
But the last part of that scripture says we should test God, and see that he will pour out such a blessing, we will not have enough room for it.

You need to understand something here, the blessing is never in the command; it is always in your obedience to the command that will produce the results. God is not dictated to by time; he doesn't start something, and then follow the processes of time. No! According to the scriptures, He knows the end from the beginning. So God is not looking to achieve something; He is wanting us to experience what He has already done. He is looking for our participation in what He has already accomplished; He just wants us to enjoy His abundant provision. So we know what the reward is already, we just need to trust and obey the command in order to get the reward.

Do you believe that in this passage God is really begging for your money? If you think that God can't do anything without your help or participation, then ask yourself this question, where were you when God was creating the world? Did God need your help? No! He created everything to perfection, established the laws and principles which govern and sustain life as we know it, then put man in the middle and said 'enjoy; have control over everything, I give it all to you my children.'

But notice this point; He did not create everything, He just created the first; then commanded it to re-create after its own kind, to reproduce.

The natural world is in perfect harmony with God's command, just by obeying God's order.

Let's put it this way; tomorrow is not another day, tomorrow is a brand new, never been before created day. No one has ever seen tomorrow because it has not yet been created. Tomorrow is actually today reproducing after its own kind. When the sun comes up in the morning, it's not because it is on a piece of string. It is following in obedience to the order that commanded it. It is operated by obedience to the command God gave on the first ever day, and it has just reproduced or re-created ever since in obedience to the first and only command it received. So we have each day and are blessed by obedience to God's command.

The only thing that has not been obedient to God is us. People in the world are suffering, perishing because we are not obeying as children of God and reproducing after our own kind. We don't follow God's command.
You know sometimes demons are more obedient than us!
Jesus never had a problem with a demon; they did exactly what Jesus told them to do every time! They obeyed his command straight away. It was those Pharisees, the educated, the supposedly chosen ones, the high priests that gave him all the problems.

Anyway, let me stick to my point before I go off on a rabbits trail. So everything works and is perfectly synchronised by obedience to Gods command.

So if you think that this passage **Malachi 3:8-10** is just God begging you for your money so that he can reach the poor, hungry and needy with the gospel, then please trust me on this; keep your money!

Hear, O my people, and I will speak, O Israel, and I will testify against you: I am God, your God. I do not rebuke you for your sacrifices or your burnt offerings, which are ever before me. I have no need of a bull from your stall or of goats from your pens, for every animal of the forest is mine, and the cattle on a thousand hills. I know every bird in the mountains, and the creatures in the field are mine. If I were hungry I will not tell you for the world is mine, and all that is in it. Do I eat the flesh of bulls or drink the blood of goats? Sacrifice thank-offerings to God, fulfil your vows to the most high, and call upon me in the day of trouble; I will deliver you, and you will honour me.
Psalm 50:7.

In this scripture, God is reminding us that He owns everything, the reason for our giving to Him, is just for us to confirm within ourselves who our God is, who we trust and rely on. It is for our own good, so that in times of trouble, we can call on Him and He will respond because we acknowledge who He is. So if you can come to the understanding that God doesn't need it, He just wants to show you that you don't need it either, all you need is His provision which comes through obedience to His word and command, then you can freely give with a cheerful heart, which is his command.

So as you give, give according to his word, with a grateful heart, with thanksgiving, with the understanding that all you have today, is purely because of His love for you.

Trust in God to provide for you.
The widow's mite.
Luke 21: 1-4

Here is a very small, but absolutely powerful picture the Bible paints for us. It has nothing to do with how much or how little we give; it is about our heart condition, the motive behind our offering.

As he looked up, Jesus saw the rich putting their gifts into the temple treasury. He also saw a poor widow put in two very small copper coins. "I tell you the truth," he said, "This poor widow has put in more than all the others. All these people gave their gifts out of their wealth; but she out of her poverty put in all she had to live on."
Luke 21: 1-4.

Here we see the rich giving out of their abundance, proudly supporting the work of God, giving freely and openly. All of which, is good. Then here comes a poor widow, she gives all she had to support the church. Wow! Could you do that? Who do you trust in?

Jesus saw that this woman gave everything she had, yet He didn't go over and bless her with more. He could have! So why didn't He? Simple, this widow showed that her trust and entire dependency was in God's ability to provide for her. She just believed and knew that God would always take care of her so giving out of her poverty was easy, because she knew God would never fail her.

Her faith was sufficient to the point that Jesus himself didn't need to go over and intervene. He was proud of her, so much that this seemingly small picture and her tiny offering, is talked about in churches around the world till today.

This also tells us that Jesus was watching what other people were giving, and what they were holding back. Where is your trust? Can you be found faithful enough to trust in God's abundant supply?

Now let's look at the other side of this coin:

Now a man came up to Jesus and asked, "Teacher, what good thing must I do to get eternal life?" "Why do you ask me about what is good?" Jesus replied. "There is only one who is good. If you want to enter life, obey the commandments." "Which ones?" The man enquired. Jesus replied, "Do not steal, do not give false testimony, honour your father and mother, and love your neighbour as yourself." "All these I have kept," the young man said. "What do I still lack?" Jesus answered, "If you want to be perfect, go, sell your possessions and give to the poor, and you will have treasure in heaven. Then come, follow me." When the young man heard this, he went away sad, because he had great wealth. Then Jesus said to his disciples, "I tell you the truth, it is hard for a rich man to enter the kingdom of heaven. Again I tell you, it is easier for a camel to pass through the eye of a needle than for a rich man to enter the kingdom of God." **Matthew 19:16-24.**

Here we see Jesus in the middle of a synagogue preaching, with people all around Him listening. This young man pushes through everyone and approaches Jesus in plain sight in order to ask his questions. From the outside, this is a show of someone who is very proud and bold. He was happy with life and how generous he was to others. He has kept all the commandments, and was very rich. Yet Jesus wasn't imprest.

A lot of people then use this scripture to bring the case that in order to enter heaven, you need to be poor, it is easier to get into heaven, because Jesus says very clearly here that, it is easier for a camel to go through the eye of a needle than for a rich man to enter into heaven.

But look at where this man's trust was; not in God! Jesus said to him, sell everything you have and give to the poor, and then you will have treasure in heaven. That was a guarantee direct from Jesus! But no! This man wanted his treasure here and now. But why did Jesus say that then? Does it mean we should all be poor? No! Jesus just wanted to put this young man back in his place, He was just showing that yes, this man has obeyed all the commandments, he has done really well for himself and family, even those around him, which is great, but Jesus knew his heart, where his trust really was. Jesus wanted to show that he was only bold and confident because he had all this wealth! He wasn't completely dependant on God.

Rich people tend to trust and rely on their wealth because they have proof of what it can do for them; but this is not the right way. We need to build our trust in God, because one day, all this worldly wealth and luxury will soon be gone! Then who will you call on?

Yes God wants you wealthy, but He doesn't want you to rely on that wealth, He wants your complete trust and foundation to be built on his provision so that you do not become consumed by what money can do for you, but what God can do through you.

Lessons from a giver (part 1)
1 kings 17:7-16

There are a lot of truths here and principles that we really need to grab hold of and study for our own good. This book is not just about showing you the evidence that God wants you wealthy. If you would really study and apply the principles to your everyday life and money, you will have the proof of what I'm saying for yourself! Then hopefully you would go out and teach others. It's about applying this Biblical principle to your finances in order to break the grip money has over you.

So these two parts I will be going into now are a revelation of my own heart; who I am, this is me all over, and I want to challenge some of you.
People say to me that I should be a bit more sensitive, I should speak a bit kinder; and I really try to sometimes, but when I study the Bible and see the type of character God is able to perform great miracles through, I find it hard to drop my standards. The people are strong, fighters, just keep getting up, warriors, ambassadors for God, people who never give up until its over, they get the job done no matter the opposition or how bad things look, they do it until its done, no complaining! This is what God looks for in a person, that's the character He can work with. I have a motto!

A man is not finished when he's defeated, a man is only finished when he quits!

Now let's study the characteristics of this widow, who truly was a giver:

Then the word of the Lord came to him: "Go at once to Zarephath of Sidon and stay there. I have commanded a widow in that place to supply you with food" so he went to Zarephath. When he came to the town gate, a widow was there gathering sticks. He called to her and asked, "Would you bring me a little water in a jar so I may have a drink?" As she was going to get it, he called, "And bring me please, a piece, of bread." "As surely as the Lord your God lives," she replied, "I don't have any bread- only a handful of flower in a jar and a little oil in a jug. I am gathering a few sticks to take home and make a meal for myself and my son that we may eat it – and die." Elijah said to her, "Don't be afraid. Go home and do as you have said. But first make a small cake of bread for me from what you have and bring it to me, and then make something for yourself and your son. For this is what the Lord, the God of Israel, says: The jar of flour will not be used up and the jug of oil will not run dry until the day the Lord gives rain on the land."
She went away and did as Elijah had told her. So there was food every day for Elijah and the woman and her family. For the jar of flour was not used up and the jug of oil did not run dry, in keeping with the word of the Lord spoken by Elijah.
1Kings 17:8-16:

Here we learn that this widow had the characteristics of a giver just by her response towards Elijah.

Not only was she a giver, but she was also a fighter, and a person who would stop what she was doing for other people. Not only that, but she is willing to obey God's command no matter what the natural outlook was.

Let's study why she was a giver. In the context of the time, there was a severe drought in the land, there was no food and people were starving to death all around. According to the beginning of this story, God had commanded her to supply someone with food. But she only had a little. She basically had a word from God, that if she gave, he would sustain her.

Elijah met her when she was gathering sticks to cook her last little bit of food for her and her son, then after that they were going to starve to death. In her eyes, this was her and her son's last day on earth.

What would you be doing if you were in this situation? Most of us would be praying, weeping, feeling sorry, and focusing on how bad things were.

This widow wasn't complaining; she wasn't locked up somewhere sulking; she was doing what she needed to do. She understood the Lord's prayer, "give us this day our daily bread" Not week, month or year. This day! She had enough food for the day so she just got on with things. In her head, she was not dead yet! Wow, I love this woman.

This is the kind of attitude God can work with, the "I'm not finished yet" attitude, I may be down; things might look bad; the future is bleak, but for now, I'm not dead yet. We need to trust him daily and just get on with things. We think too much sometimes; we focus and magnify the negatives a lot; remember Moses at the red sea, he got down on his knees and started praying, God said "what are you doing? Get up! Stretch out your staff and walk through the water". You can't sit down, get depressed and start moaning every time you come against an obstacle; stand up and get on with it! God won't move you; but he will move with you.

Elijah asked the widow for water. In those days it wasn't a matter of just turning on a tap, they had wells to draw from. She had to drop the sticks she was gathering, stop what she was doing for herself, go to the well, and draw water from it to give to this stranger.

Now ask yourself honestly, would you do that? Remember, it is you and your son's last day on earth, would you drop what you were doing for someone else?
What if it was your best day on earth?
This character the widow displayed proves she was a giver. Other people's needs were important to her. She wasn't just thinking about herself and her situation, but she still cared for others. She had a giving heart and that is why God could use her for this mighty miracle. She was still willing to serve, to give in spite of how things were looking. You see, to be a giver is not just about money, it's a heart condition. A lot of the time when we talk about giving, people immediately associate it with money. No! Smiling is a form of giving, speaking positive words to people, spending time, and talking with others that need someone, are also forms of giving. Think about others, bless them in their needs. As you give, it shall be given unto you, not just money.

There is a reason certain people see miracles. Elijah asked for bread, she basically said, "you know my heart, I would love to give, but I don't have much". Elijah said, "God will supply your needs, just make mine first, you will not run out of food if you give to me the first fruits".

The problem today is we are always waiting for more; until we have a lot for ourselves, then we can start giving and being generous. You will miss out on your miracle, in fact, with a mentality like that, you are not ready for God's provision, and we delay our blessing by looking only at our situation. It is in the little that God builds our faith and dependency on Him. And thank God, because that's all we have; a little; so this is a great place to start, we are already ready. Begin with the small you have, it's not too late; you will be preparing yourself for a miracle. Prove God in your giving; only He can multiply what you have right now!

Lessons from a giver (part 2)
1 kings 17:17-24

In the first part, we explored the attitude or characteristics if you will, of this widow. She truly was a giver; even on her last day on earth, her lowest point, she was still willing to share the little she had. She wasn't at home crying; begging God for more! She had her bread for that day so she just got on with things. This brought her into the path of Elijah where she was challenged to give to the man of God first.

Now let's study the results of her character. If you have a pastor or spiritual father, someone you can call on in times of real need, someone who you believe has that close connection with God, they feed you the word of God, they help you grow in the scriptures; do you truly appreciate them?

Pastors do an awesome job; in fact, they have the hardest job in the world because first of all, they are dealing with people. Any other occupation focuses on one main area. A rocket scientist only has to worry about rocket science; a surgeon only has to worry about surgery and so on. But a pastor has to be extremely versatile, multitalented. They have to be a pastor, father figure, marriage counsellor, youth worker, motivator, shoulder to cry on, financial adviser and family man, a patient and understanding person; the list goes on and on.

So when was the last time you personally showed him or her gratitude? Proved that you are truly grateful for all their hard work? When was the last time you encouraged them? You supported them financially, gave a gift? When did you last bless them? Or do you just think they don't need it and move on? Believe me; it is for your own personal benefit to show your gratitude, also, trust me they need your support and encouragement. It is not an easy calling.

You know there are certain things a pastor would find it hard to preach about, because of our human emotions, we start drawing conclusions; but if you ever feel like someone is preaching just to get your money, then please, keep your money!

But I'm not a pastor so I can give it to you straight. I will show you as it is because you need to see this; these are Biblical principles which are laid out for our own benefit.

Back to the story, there was a drought, this widow used the little bit of nothing she had to support the man of God and in doing so, she proved that God is an awesome and a miraculous God. Through the man of God, she was building up faith in God's supply through him. They were sustained throughout the drought.

So look what happened during the course of Elijah's ministry.

Some time later the son of the woman who owned the house became ill. He grew worse and worse, and finally stopped breathing. She said to Elijah, "what do you have against me, man of God? Do you come to remind me of my sin and kill my son?" "Give me your son" Elijah replied, he took him from her arms, carried him to the upper room where he was staying, and laid him on his bed. Then he cried out to the Lord, "O Lord my God, have you brought tragedy also on this widow I am staying with, by causing her son to die?" Then he stretched himself out on the boy three times and cried to the Lord, "O Lord my God, let this boy's life return to him!" The Lord heard Elijah's cry, and the boy's life returned to him, and he lived. Elijah picked up the child and carried him down from the room into the house. He gave him to his mother and said, "Look, your son is alive!" Then the woman said to Elijah, "Now I know that you are a man of God and that the word of God from your mouth is the truth."
1Kings 17:17-24:

This widow's son grew ill and died. What a tragedy, the death of a child must have been devastating to her as it was her only son. But yet again, instead of sitting down and crying; having a pity party for herself; focusing on the negative of how bad things were, she brought her dead son to Elijah and basically said, " you sort this out." She had no Idea what would happen, all she knew was that God had performed a mighty miracle through this man of God before, so she just asked for help.

Elijah prayed to God on her behalf. Elijah had built up a special relationship with this widow because of her willingness to support him, her character, and her continued support of his ministry. Elijah prayed earnestly for the child, he didn't even know what would happen. All he knew was this woman needed help in some way. He didn't even know if this boy could be brought back to life. All he wanted to do was repay her in some way for her kind support. He prayed and the boy came back from the dead!

You know, this principle here, of directly supporting or blessing a minister, is for your own benefit. If you notice, this was actually the first time a person has ever been raised from the dead in the history of the Bible. In fact, her son was the first person in the world, to be raised from the dead! Elijah had no recollection of anyone being raised from the dead. Up until this point, when some one died, they were dead! No coming back. Jesus was not even born yet, so Elijah wasn't following or operating with the same power Jesus had to raise people from the dead. Elijah just knew that he had to try something to comfort this widow in her time of distress. Because of that bond the widow had built up with Elijah, the minister of God, in the long run, what she gained was worth a lot more than money could ever buy.

From this story here, we should learn that, it's not always about money; it's about building our faith in God and His power working through people. So that in our crisis, we would have already proved that God can do all things through His ministers.

Today, I encourage you to support your minister financially and otherwise, show them you love them; you are grateful, even begin to thank God for their life, bless your minister with what you have. In so doing you might even be preparing yourself for a great miracle.

Your Heavenly account; supporting a minister of God
Philippians 4: 14-20

There is one thing we should try to all be clear about, and it is the fact that no matter how much wealth we accumulate here on earth, we can not take any of it with us. All this stuff will one day be all burnt up. But did you know there is a heavenly account where you can actually send money? If you believe this, would you want to know how you can make small deposits there? And how would you start allocating your use of money? Let's see what the Bible says about this fact:

Yet it was good for you to share in my troubles. Moreover, as you Philippians know, in the early days of your acquaintance with the gospel, when I set out from Macedonia, not one church shared with me in the matter of giving and receiving, except you only; for even when I was in Thessalonica, you sent me aid again and again when I was in need. Not that I am looking for a gift, but I am looking for what may be credited into your account. I have received full payment and even more; I am amply supplied, now that I have received from epaphroditus the gifts you sent. They are a fragrant offering, an acceptable sacrifice, pleasing to God. And my God will meet all your needs according to his glorious riches in Christ Jesus. To our God and Father be glory for ever and ever. Amen.
Philippians 4: 14-20.

This is part of a letter Paul writes to the church of the Philippians which he started. I would strongly urge you to study the book of Philippians in your own time. It will benefit you greatly.

The portion I would like us to focus on at this point, is in verse seventeen where Paul reveals to us that there is an account in heaven, where our gifts, offerings and support to a minister or ministry is being recorded; *"Not that I am looking for a gift, but I am looking for what may be credited to your account."*

This is great as it shows clearly that what you do here on earth can actually prepare a place for you in heaven; so when people say you cant take your money with you when you die, this portion of scripture actually counteracts that mentality by teaching us, you can't take it with you, but you can actually send it ahead of you. Your use of money today, can affect your future, even your eternal dwelling, by directly supporting a man or woman of God.

You know, a pastor's work is to feed us the immutable, unchangeable word of God; to help guide us into a closer relationship with Jesus Christ. But let's imagine; your pastor is in your shoes, with your financial burdens, they are always worrying about money and how they would get through each month, just relying on one income stream. It would be hard for them to operate in the fullness of their ability if he or she was constantly worrying about money.

So when you give directly to a minister, you are in a sense freeing up more time in their mind in support for you, they can pray more for your future needs.

Here is another scripture which states that your money can be sent ahead of you, proving the case of a heavenly account, this time taught by Jesus.

Do not store up for yourselves treasures on earth, where rust and month destroy, and where thieves break in and steal. But store up for yourselves treasures in Heaven, where rust and moth do not destroy, and where thieves do not break in and steal. For where your treasure is, there your heart will be also.
Matthew 6: 19-21.

This portion shows, not only is it possible to send your money ahead of you, but it also proves to God where your heart is. The last part says that where your heart truly is, that's where most of your money will go. So today, check your spending pattern; where does most of your money go? Because let's face it, that's where your heart is. If you are in debt, and most your money is going on servicing those debts, your heart desires on what ever you borrowed that money for, is what put you in that situation. How are you prioritising your spending? According to this scripture, where your heart is, that's where your treasure is. Is your treasure in heaven or here on earth and in worldly things which thieves can steal it?

Lastly, allow me the opportunity to show you one more way of investing money aside for your future use.

Give generously to him and do so without a grudging heart; then because of this the Lord your God will bless you in all your work and all you put your hand to. There will always be poor people in the land. Therefore I command you to be open handed towards your brothers and towards the poor and needy in your land.
Deuteronomy 15: 10-11.

Giving to the poor generously and with the right heart, will cause God's blessings upon your work.

He who is kind to the poor lends to the Lord, and he will reward him for what he has done.
Proverbs 19:17.

These two scriptures verify that giving freely, motivated by love and a good heart condition actually has an affect on your future.

Here God says giving to the poor is actually lending money to the Lord. Who would you like to lend money to?

So as you sit down to make your plans for the future, it would be wise to incorporate giving freely, not only to the poor and needy but also to support the pastor and his or her ministry. This is definitely a wise use of your money according to the Bible.

General offering talk
Deuteronomy 8:18

But thy shalt remember the Lord thy God: for it is he that giveth thee power to get wealth, that he may establish his covenant which he sware unto thy fathers, as it is this day.
Deuteronomy 8:18.

You should notice from this passage alone, it has nothing to do with money, it is all about power! Ability. Most real born again, true believers in the gospel of Jesus would love to go out and feed the hungry. We would all love to provide for orphans, needy people, the helpless. We have the desire to want to help others less fortunate than us. The church has the vision to reach out to a hurting world. We want to spread the gospel and see people set free from mental bondage, financial struggles and so on. And these are all good things aren't they? These are all life-changing for the better desires. So you see there is no lack of good ideas, motives or the want to do these things. But how many of us know that's not good enough!
You can't help the hungry if you're hungry! You can't give to the needy if you're in need!
What is lacking is the power or the ability to achieve these goals, to fulfil these ambitions. In most cases, it requires money in order to achieve it. So as long as the enemy can keep us poor in our thinking, we will never achieve and reach those lost souls.

One of the ways to reach them is to give to a local church, fund it as it were.

Let me just say this quickly, if you ever think someone is talking just to get your money, then you should keep your money. But if you feel in your heart that you like what is going on in your local church, you like the ideas the Church has and what they have been doing, and you want to support it financially because you think it is a good work, then your offering will be accepted, no matter how big or small, because the motive behind your giving is more important than what you actually give.

So please, don't ever feel under any pressure to give, just go with your heart's desire, you are loved either way.

So to those who want to give freely, you should do it according to the word of God, with a cheerful heart, don't kiss your money goodbye, it will be going to help spread the good news of Jesus Christ to a hurting world.

Now that's the best use of your money! You know the system of this world is flawed, it is pointless, you work hard, make money, buy material things, save up, then one day you die and give it all away. You see, it doesn't work!

But when you give generously to a church, the money is used to help people, give them hope, and change their lives for the better. Now that is positive use however you look at it!

It is He who has given you the ability to produce wealth.

Man shall not live by bread alone.
Mathew 4:4

As we come into this second portion of this book, we will be studying the fact that God has said in His word, that He has already given us the ability to produce wealth. The ability is within us. But what is wealth? Wealth is different from rich. Rich means you can pay all your bills, go on nice holidays, have fancy things and spend lots of Quality time with your friends and family. That's all good. But wealth is a whole other level. Wealth is all the benefits of rich, but wealth, gives you the power to make others rich. A multi millionaire who is an entrepreneur is wealthy, his directors and all those close to him who have benefited from him, are rich. That's the difference.

Wealth according to the dictionary means:
- An abundance of valuable material possessions or resources.
- A great amount
- The state of being affluent
- A large possession
- Having a plentiful supply of material, goods and money.

Rich is given to you by someone else but wealth is produced from within you. Wealth means you having the resources.

God does not make mistakes, He does not love one person more than another, He does not accidentally bless someone when He meant to bless another, I am not blessed by mistake, I am not financially stable by accident, and nothing takes God by surprise!

Ever since becoming a Christian, I have tried to live according to the word of God (to the best of my ability) and am now reaping the benefits which are associated with obeying Gods commands. I trust and obey!

So this portion of scripture teaches me a lot:

Jesus answered, "it is written: Man does not live on bread alone, but on every word that comes from the mouth of God"
Matthew 4:4

Here is more proof that the word of God, if you are obedient to it, will literally feed you; it will put food on your table. It will take care of you and sustain you through hard times no matter what. You can live by the word of God. You know, you can actually live on bread alone, but you will be malnourished, you won't have a good life, your health will deteriorate, so basically, you will just be existing. When God says live, He is talking about having the fullness of life. A good, balanced, exciting, 'worth waking up in the morning for' life. There are lessons and principles for everyday living. If these are applied to your own life, you too will be fulfilled.

This is what the Lord says – your redeemer, the Holy one of Israel: "I am the Lord your God, who teaches you to profit, who directs you in the way you should go."
Isaiah 48:17.

God will teach you to profit! To prosper from the word of God, you need to obey the commands! You can't just do it one week when all is going well, then when things get hard, or life deals us a bad hand we fall flat on our faces and just give up. No! We need to be strong, stand up and keep going, Obey God no matter how bad things might be looking in the natural!

Carefully follow the terms of this covenant, so that you may prosper in everything you do.
Deuteronomy 29:9.

If we just study the word of God, keep His commands, do and apply the principles, we will be prosperous. The word of God makes us righteous, and then God blesses the righteous.

The blessing of the Lord brings wealth and He adds no trouble to it.
Proverbs 10:22.

Only the blessing of God can truly make you wealthy without having problems.

Your mentality has to be right, money can actually cause you more problems than you could have ever imagined. Just ask the rich about their experiences.

73

Remember that the Bible is the book that ever sold the most in history; people today are still using it and reaping the benefits of the words written in it. The Bible holds so many truths. I even heard that in the 1960s Dale Carnegie actually called it the blueprint for business. Many companies have applied the principles outlined in regards to handling money; they have become very successful and even adapted the words from the Bible into their own company motto.

If you take your time to study this book, it will undoubtedly open your understanding to why it is God wants you wealthy, and then you will be able to rely on these principles as the truth.

It is He who has given you the ability to produce wealth.

Where there is no vision the people perish!
Proverbs 29:18

A lot of the time as Christians, we don't rely on the fact that the Bible in its entirety is written for our benefit. We sometimes take certain parts and leave out others.
So now let's look into the area of your vision: your God-given dream.
Do you have a vision? A goal or a dream?

Why do you get up every morning and go to work? Why do you do what you do? What are you aiming for? A lot of us are aiming at nothing and hitting it every time! Now if you have no vision, according to this passage, you will perish.

Where there is no vision, the people perish: But he that keepeth the law, happy is he.
Proverbs 29:18.

A vision is basically a dream, something to look forward to that excites you.

It's like when you have a great holiday booked. You constantly think about it, what it would be like when your there. The things you are going to do, how you would relax under the sun. You have no work to do and so on. Though it is in the future, whenever you come across a tough situation or are having a bad day, you just think on your holiday and that helps you get through. I hope this is making sense.

You have something exciting to look forward to, so you don't really allow the present circumstance to ruin your mood. Also, your spending pattern changes, you start to put money aside for the holiday, you start buying things that will be suitable for the holiday, and you put things in place in case things go wrong. You plan for the holiday. Though you are in the present, your mind is on something great in the future. This is a vision.

The second part of the scripture reveals to us that there are laws which are associated with having a vision. In other words, if you have a vision, dream or goal, in order to achieve the vision, you have to be guided by certain laws, or be governed by the laws which will lead you to the end result. Let's use a simple example; if you wanted to be an Olympic swimmer, you need to train at the standard that will make you an Olympic swimmer! That is the law which guides that dream! If you don't train, you won't be one! How simple is that? You have to set certain routines, cut out things in your life style that don't add value to you becoming a great swimmer, and add things that help you become a better swimmer.

Your whole lifestyle has to revolve around you training to become an Olympic swimmer. You set laws for yourself that require you do them whether you feel up to it or not. There is so much to this that I don't really want to dwell on it too much, you should by now understand that a law means you do it. The Bible says happy is he that finds the law to the vision.

So get your self a vision, write it down, note the different steps and stages you need to go through in order to achieve it, and then stick to them until your reach the goal.

Be sure to evaluate your progress along the way, give yourself a little pat on the back when you have reached a set mile stone. Even God did this each day during creation to teach us to look back on our progress.

And God said "let the waters under the heaven be gathered together unto one place, and let the dry land appear": and it was so.
And God called the dry land Earth; and the gathering together of the waters called the Seas: and God saw that it was good.
Genesis 1:9-10

Another part of this is to recognise what has not been done well. This way, you can find a solution:

The Lord God said "it is not good for man to be alone. I will make a helper suitable for him."
Genesis 2:18

Now we understand that God Himself could have created the entire world and all within it in just one day. So why did it take Him 5 days?

This is to teach us how to do things in order, with a bigger picture in mind. He is teaching us a pattern for creating something that is sustainable and long lasting.

A normal or routine working life will always try to kill that dream you have, it will always bring you down to where you feel unfulfilled, so you need something to hold onto, an anchor as it were, something to be working towards. You need a good reason for waking up every morning, something that drives you, brings meaning to your every day existence because without one, you are just a slave to money.

Money tells you what to do, when to wake up, when to go to sleep, when you can take a holiday and when you can't afford to. Let's be real, money rules a lot of us.

Understand that God gets no glory out of that! He doesn't get excited that we are just a machine waking up the same time every day, just stuck in a routine like the rest of the world just forming an existence hoping nothing takes us by surprise.

So what are you working towards? Why do you do it? It should definitely not just be to accumulate worldly possessions, just look at this scripture:

Man is a mere phantom as he goes to and fro: he bustles about, but only in vain; he heaps up wealth, not knowing who will get it.
Psalm 39:6.

This scripture is a stark reminder that we are not here for very long! And that we can't take anything with us. So why do we do it? Why do we surround ourselves with so many material things which are here today gone tomorrow?

Why does the Bible say you need a dream? Simple, it helps you to deal with what is going on right now in the present because you know there is something greater ahead of you worth striving for. It helps ground you, keeps you going, and it will cause you not to focus on all the problems right now because your focus will be on the end goal. It helps you stop making rash decisions and spontaneous purchases, because you can align your thoughts with what you are aiming for.

Write down your goal and routinely evaluate your progress. Note down the different stages you need to get to. Set daily, weekly, monthly and yearly goals and stages to evaluate your progress so that you can keep track of how you're doing.
If you don't know where you're going, there is no way of telling where you are!

I meet people all the time, when I ask what their goal is, they almost start by saying, I want to be debt free. That is good, but not really a good dream. "How did you get into debt in the first place?" Would always be my next question. You see the world advertises to us so expertly how good our life would be if we just had every creature comfort right now. Buy now pay later as it were.

But we tend to forget it needs to be paid back later. In most cases, with a lot more interest, so we go off and buy more on credit until it spirals out of control then we wind up wandering how to get out of this situation, then we start to fantasise what life would be like if we were debt free. That seems backwards because you were debt free before you got into debt, now you want to visualise yourself back when you were debt free? That's not really looking forward, that's looking backwards.

I hope I haven't offended anyone but lets be real about this! If you got a pay rise today, your income doubled, did you know most of us would just run out and double our monthly outgoings to suite our new income. After a while we then realise that we are still in the same situation but this time just more money coming in and more going out.

Let me try and help here a little bit. First of all there is such a thing as good debt as well as there is bad debt. Money borrowed to buy something which is increasing in value, is good debt, but money borrowed to buy things that are decreasing in value, or unnecessary worldly pleasures, that's bad debt.
But since we are talking about having a vision, we would all love to be debt free regardless of how we got there in the first place. Debt freedom is good because let me tell you from experience, money does not guarantee you happiness, but debt can definitely afford you misery.
If you're thinking that money can buy you happiness, then please answer me this question. Why do we see a lot of wealthy Hollywood actors & actresses, music stars and so called celebrities, with a lot of money struggling with depression, sleepless nights, drug abuse, alcohol addiction and so on?

You see if you're not happy and fulfilled inside, no matter how much money you make, it will not satisfy you. We need to work on our insides first, before we start using money to pretty up or outsides.
Anyway, let's say we have a vision of becoming debt free, you need to apply the Biblical principle here of finding the law of that dream.

We need to establish the law, then stick to the rules, steps and stages that would get us to realise the vision. Seek help, be honest, there is no point struggling with debt and trying to look like everything is ok in front of other church folk. Believe me; a lot of them are in the same situation as you are. We are supposed to help each other! Not deceive each other. You know there are a lot of people in life that will lie to you! Why lie to yourself as well?

You begin by writing down (honestly) how much debt you have. Next you write down the monthly payments for each debt. Then you find out the APR for the debts. The rule is to then learn to budget; then focus on paying off one debt at a time (always the debt with the highest APR) So you pay as little as you can to the other debts, then increase the amount you pay to the one with the highest APR. When that one is paid off, you release the monthly payments from that one, and you then focus on the one that has the second highest APR. You work your way down from that till it is all paid off. Now if you have this plan written down, you would be able to calculate how long it will take you to become debt free. But it will only happen if you stick to your plan, no impulse purchases, don't add more debt in order to pay off too quickly. Stick to your plan, it will definitely help you.

Back to having a vision aside from becoming debt free, the way I get people to search for a vision or dream is; I get them to pray and seek God honestly for a Kingdom vision and purpose. Then you have to sit back and find out what you really enjoy doing, what you do well with minimum effort.

Get ready to receive: Imagine you have no responsibilities in life, no debt or bills to pay and a minimum of forty thousand pounds in the bank; cash.

Now ask God what you should do!

This only works if your heart is right with God. If you get the idea to go on a holiday and spend it all, then that is not from God. If you get the sudden urge to gamble in order to multiply it, then I doubt that your heart is in the right place.

You can tell if you get a God given, Kingdom inspired vision! Your heart will start racing, your emotions will become overwhelmed, and you can picture yourself there doing those things. Most of all, it will give you drive and passion; you can then begin to align your daily life with the vision and bring meaning to your every day existence.

The labourer's appetite works for him; his hunger drives him on.
Proverbs 16:26.

This here tells us that when you have a vision that you really want to achieve, don't worry about how hard it might get, if you really want it, that passion, that hunger for it will drive you. You will have strength from somewhere.

You know when you're passionate about something; you look forward to doing it. It's not hard to you. Others might say how do you do that so effortlessly? Its simple, your passion and hunger is the driving force behind you.

So why not go for it? Today, get a vision, write it down and begin to align yourself, family work and business up with it.

It is He who has given you the ability to produce wealth.

Where there is no vision the people perish!
(Part 2)
Proverbs 29:18

In the first part of this portion we saw how important it is to have a vision, because according to this passage; we will perish without one. A vision can also be described as a dream or goal. A goal helps you to stay focused on the end result and keeps you from being consumed by daily problems which just try to kill your dreams.
Now let's take our time to really explore this idea of having a vision.

He who works his land will have abundant food, but he who chases fantasies lacks judgement.
Proverbs 12:11.

The first part talks about working your land, in other words, what you already have. The second part is describing having a realistic goal. You know it is good to have a dream, but if it is not realistic, it's just a fantasy.

This is great because it is basically saying, now you have a dream, you need to do it! You have to go and work for it, put your plan into action. You write it down, evaluate the different steps you need to take in order to reach the main goal, what you have to change in your life; the different skills you need to acquire; the people you need to associate with and those you need to draw away from.

Do not surround yourself with negative people who are always looking on the dark side of life. Instead, find people who are like-minded, those who challenge you to keep reaching higher, to keep going.

Surround yourself with winners, people who do! Not just talk! That way their enthusiasm for life will keep you motivated. You know if you want to be a football player, you don't spend most of your time around fishermen. No, you try to spend more time around those players who are better than you because you need to be challenged. You need to be associated with the players that play professionally; they have skills you can learn, they have experience of the game already, and they sharpen you. Whatever your vision is, get around those that enhance you within that field. You don't always need to be teaching others, sometime you need to be taught. You need to better yourself.

Now if your vision is not written down, you will not be able to guage how you are doing in order to reach that goal! Life circumstances change constantly and priorities always take you by surprise. If your vision is not written, it becomes a moving target, you are tossed too and fro by life's dictates, but when your vision is written, all the steps are set, you can go back to it periodically and remind yourself of what it is you are working for. It will remind you to get up and keep going. It is the easiest thing in the world to give up, to quit. But it is the hardest thing to decide to keep fighting on!

How can you know that you are progressing towards your goals if they are not written? How can you guage your success?

This is a Biblical principle that even the banks and business world require of you. Why do you think companies have a business plan? When starting up a business, if you need funding from the bank, the first thing they require from you is your business plan. What is your vision for this business?

So even in the world today, a lot of Biblical principles are in operation; helping and aiding unbelievers. How ironic that there are Christians who think they are too busy to study the Bible: working to pay their bills.

You need a vision! Then you need to work it in order to achieve it. I see a lot of Christians who get a vision, a quick burst of ambition or motivation, an idea. They just run out and tell everyone that will listen, who in turn get excited for them; they start believing they can achieve it, get excited at the thought of it and talk about what they are going to do and achieve with God's help. But guess what? God can't help your talk! He can't guide you if you're not moving! If you're not doing something! They say talk is cheap, but the Bible puts it this way.

All hard work brings a profit, but mere talk leads only to poverty.
Proverbs 14:23.

Now that's very blunt. It doesn't say talk is cheap, it says it will actually lead you into poverty.

This is the reason I have written this book, to show that it is not just about having great ambitions, good visions and Godly motivated goals, it's about evidence! Prove it! Achieve it! Do it! You've got a dream? Do it! What are you doing to achieve it? What are you cutting back on?

How are you disciplining yourself? How are you measuring your success? How are you using your time? What is the majority of your money going on? Do you even know where your money is going? Write your vision down and align yourself and your life up with that end goal.

So to sum up, you need a vision, then you write it down and stick to it. In my last venture we had a saying, *"plan your work, then work your plan"*
But now in the Bible or with the Kingdom principles, I have learnt my new motto.

Only those who do the work, get the reward!

The parable of the Talents.

Matthew 25:14-30

Again, it will be like a man going on a journey, who called his servants and entrusted his property to them. To one he gave five talents of money, to another two talents, and to another one talent, each according to his ability. Then he went on his Journey. The man who had received five talents went at once and put his money to work and gained five more. So also, the one with the two talents gained two more. But the man who had received the one talent went off, dug a whole in the ground and hid his masters' money.

After a long time the master of those servants returned and settled accounts with them. The man who received the five talents brought the other five. "Master," he said, "you entrusted me with five talents. See, I have gained five more."

His master replied, "Well done, good and faithful servant! You have been faithful with a few things; I will put you in charge of many things. Come and share your master's happiness!"

Also the man who received two talents brought the other two. "Master," he said, "you entrusted me with two talents. See, I have gained two more."

His master replied, "Well done, good and faithful servant! You have been faithful with a few things;

I will put you in charge of many things. Come and share your master's happiness!"

Then the man who had received the one talent came. "Master," he said, "I knew that you are a hard man, harvesting where you did not sow and gathering where you have not scattered seed. So I was afraid and went out and hid your money in the ground. See, here is what belongs to you."

His master replied, "you wicked, lazy servant! So you knew I harvest where I have not sown and gather where I have not scattered seed? Well then, you should have put my money on deposit with the bankers, so that when I returned I would have received it back with interest. Take the talent from him and give it to the one who has the ten talents. For everyone who has will be given more, and he will have an abundance. Whoever does not have, even what he has will be taken from him. And throw that worthless servant outside, into the darkness, where there will be weeping and gnashing of teeth."

It is He who has given you the ability to produce wealth.

The parable of the talents: Part 1
Matthew 25:14-30

This parable is an awesome teaching by Jesus which hits the nail on the head in regards to our view and use of money. It has such a wide range of lessons, that we can apply any of these principles to our finances and get the same results.

You are free to read the parable in its entirety for yourself if you wish, but I will be breaking it down into five parts so we can study the principles step by step to get a full understanding of what Jesus is trying to say.

Again, it will be like a man going on a journey, who called his servants and entrusted his property to them. To one he gave five talents of money, to another two talents, and to another one talent, each according to his ability. Then he went on his Journey.
Matthew 25:14-30:

The first and most important lesson to learn here is that each servant was giving a set amount of money, according to their ability.

What does this mean? It simply indicates that the master knew his servants individually. He knew their character and the nature or what their heart was like. He knew what their work ethic was and how much each servant would be able to handle, based on their track record.

Now lets apply this to you, what type of a worker are you? Do you only give a good day's work when the boss or manager is around? Do you constantly complain and moan about working? About your job, work colleagues, life, journey to work?

How much value does your company get from you? Do you always seem to keep job hunting? Do you start off in a new job excited but then as time goes by you get comfortable and start moaning again? When was the last time you read the organisation's mission statement? Do you even know what the organisation's values are, or even what they really do? Do you know what your position brings to the company as a whole? Are they getting their money's worth out of your employment? If you left would you be missed, or would your colleagues be glad you're gone? Do you bring the whole room down when you walk in with your negative attitude and miserable face as if the whole world is on your shoulders? Would the place be happier without you? If the answer to any of these statements is yes, then you are definitely not ready for what God has in store. You need to take your job very seriously; you know we spend most of our lives at work, so we need to make it a pleasurable experience. You can actually prove to God that you can handle more responsibility in His house by how you handle your position at work. We need to understand that what ever job we do; we need to be the best at it. You need to do it to the best of your ability, so that when you look back on the day's work, you get a real sense of satisfaction. I don't care how much you hate your job; you need to change your attitude towards how you work. Do it for yourself and God, be proud of how you work.

When ever a promotion comes up, don't you know the managers know exactly who to offer it to? It won't go to someone who is always complaining and thinking they are doing the company a favour by turning up each day. No! It will go to some one who has proved that they are worth giving more responsibility to. How you work and your attitudes are being constantly evaluated, not just by man, but also by God.

He is looking for those He can entrust with true riches.
This is verified in this passage:

If you have not been trustworthy with someone else's property, who will give you property of your own?
Luke 16:12.

There needs to be a change in character, your work ethic is the building block, where you prove to God that you can handle the true riches. Work is something we need to do in order to survive, so we should make the most of it. Be thankful that you have a job in the first place. You know we spend most of our lives at work. Lets do it like the Messiah is our employer.

Whatever your hand finds to do, do it with all your might, for in the grave, where you are going, there is neither working nor planning nor knowledge nor wisdom.
Ecclesiastes 9:10.

*A man can do nothing better than to eat and drink
and find satisfaction in his work. This too, I see, is
from the hand of God*
Ecclesiastes 3:24.

This is very simple, you have what you have worked
for, and God is not going to increase those who are
not ready.

Remember this is Jesus telling this parable, so this
shows that it applies to us today. What you have in
your hands is based on your track record, it is
according to your ability, the choices you have
made regarding your use or misuse of money, how
you work or don't work for it, how much you value
money and your understanding of how to spend it
wisely or foolishly. You have been in control all
along.

If you are one of those people who keeps praying
for more money, constantly begging for a pay rise
or to win the lottery and constantly borrowing, then
you will always remain in that state.

The parable states first, each man was given
according to his ability. In other words, even if you
receive more, as long as your ability to handle or
use it remains the same, you will just end up back
where you started. Needing more.

This is very simple, but most of us overlook this
point. The issue is not how much or how little we
have, the issue is how we use or value what we
have.

The great news is that today, you can start a fresh, a
new chapter in your life; you still have the
opportunity to change your perspective of money.

You need to begin by understanding how money works, you need to be found faithful with the little you have in your hands already before God can begin to increase the flow.

Sometimes we can gain too much too quickly and all that does is just destroy us.

There was a programme that used to air from time to time about lottery winners and what they did with their millions. For 80% of those who won the lottery, it turned out to be the worst thing that ever happened to them. It had a devastating effect on their lives. It brought nothing but grief; all their friends started begging them for money, their families just expected the same, began arguing why they gave more to one and less to another and so on. Most of the winners then had to move away from it all and tried to make new friends. The problem with that was they couldn't really relate to wealthy people who had worked hard to make their fortune. The lottery winners had just come into money through no work of their own skill.

They couldn't make new poor friends because they wouldn't get to enjoy their money in front of them. So they became isolated in a new area and were missing their old friends and lifestyle when things made sense. Depression started to set in, they began regretting the day they won the lottery, started arguing with each other, it just went on and on. In some cases, people have even taken their own lives purely because they got too much too quickly and they didn't value it.

Gaining things too quickly without effort is not a Godly principle. You should grow and multiply according to your ability to handle things.

But while I've got the lottery in my hands now, let me just expose a few things regarding it and the Christian faith.

Statistics show that the majority of the people who play the lottery are below the poverty line or just above it. The rest who play are middle income families who are just wishful thinkers. See there is a pattern here, the lottery is seen as a quick and very easy way of having your dreams come true. It looks simple; all we have to do is match the right numbers, that's it, instant millions.

That sounds very lazy to me. When you speak to those who play the lottery, you ask them, "What would you do if you won?" for the majority, the response is always the same. "I would quit work, go on a long holiday, buy a big house, fast cars, designer clothes" and so on, all I I I. It is very self motivated, what I can do to satisfy my own desires. That's not godly either.

Christians should be unselfish and care about other people. We should not gamble. All gambling is, is trying to win for yourself what everyone else has put in. Hoping to win as long as everyone else looses. We should want everyone to prosper. But the lottery winner only wins because everyone else loses. Suppose everyone chose the same winning number, then everyone would win a few pence. How many people would rejoice if that happened?

When someone buys a lottery ticket they are hoping that nobody else wins so they can have all the money for themselves. This is not in alignment with the 9th commandment "Don't covet". There is nothing wrong in admiring your neighbour's car, thinking how nice it would be to have one the same, and working towards buying a nice car. Coveting is wanting to have your neighbour's car, depriving him of it. The story is told of a man who was granted 3 wishes. The catch was that his neighbour would get double. The man asked for a fortune. He got it, but his neighbour got twice as much. He asked for a beautiful house. He got it, but his neighbour got one twice as big. So the man asked to go blind in one eye. Coveting is feeling resentful when others prosper. Love is rejoicing when others rejoice

Rejoice with those who rejoice; Mourn with those who mourn.
Romans 12:15

We should try and share in each others emotions. Have a genuine care and support system for one another. You know all this technology we have to keep in touch is no substitute for the human touch.

But why do those who have money not play the lottery? Well it's simple. The odds of winning the lottery are around 14 million to 1. These odds remain the same when there is a rollover and the jackpot is bigger. People, who have worked hard for their money, value it, even if it's just one pound, they won't just risk it for ridiculous odds like that. That's crazy.

Why work hard for your money then just give some of it away hoping that you would be that one person who wins. If you ask people who play the lottery on a regular basis, most of them don't even know or account for how much of their hard earned cash they have actually given away to the lottery. They just play it as some fantasy, something to give them hope.

Are you the type of person who is looking for a quick and easy way to true financial independence like a loser does? Or are you a person who would get up, rely on your own hard work and do what needs to be done?

You are given according to your ability. What you have now, is all you can handle. Work it! Prove you are capable of handling more, then get ready to start receiving and growing.

It is He who has given you the ability to produce wealth.

The parable of the talents: Part 2
Matthew 25:14-30

As we continue looking at this parable, in part one we saw that each man was given a set amount according to his own ability. We learnt it shows that our track record and work performance with using what we already have will determine what we will get. So your use of money today will determine your future. We also learnt that if you don't value work and what it takes to earn a living, you will just keep looking for the easy option and play the lottery or gambling, but we saw that that gaining money in this manner can actually bring more grief than our dreams coming true.

So now let's study what each man did with what he was entrusted with:

The man who had received five talents went at once and put his money to work and gained five more. So also, the one with the two talents gained two more.
Matthew 25:16-17.

Here is a very important point, these two servants were both entrusted with what they could handle and it states that they both put their money to work. That is absolutely awesome, the Bible says you can put your money to work, or in other words, you can get your money to work for you. Just think about that, you can get your money to work for you, just as hard as you work for it.

This is a very intelligent way of viewing money, not just squandering it on things that constantly depreciate in value, but spending or putting it in places that increase in value.

The first man was given five talents, he went off, put it to work and gained five more, that's a one hundred percent increase on what he was given. The second man also put his two talents to work and gained one hundred percent increase.

So today ask yourself this, how much value for money are you getting? What is the rate of return on what you have worked so hard for?

This book is not about making money, but the heart is, what are you doing with what you have?
How are you spending it? How do you work for it? How do you value it?
It's not about how much money you have, but how much money has you. Are you able to make your money increase?
Notice the things that depreciate rapidly; cars, big screen TVs, mobile phones, gadgets and gizmos. These are the things the world encourages us to spend our money on; this is also what the world uses to measure a person's success. How much your car costs, how big your TV is and so on. So we are trying to keep up with our neighbours by squandering our money on these things which are depreciating. But the man at the top of the companies which produce these things, his money is invested wisely and increasing. Which one is smart?

The things of this world are backwards and will cause you to fail if you conform to them! Don't keep spending on things that devalue. If your money is always going on, or you give priority to, things that have no resale value, God is not going to honour that, come on! God is not going to bless our stupidity.

He will not pour into a bucket which has holes, you first have to take time and fix the holes, and then you pour into it.

Now I'm not saying you shouldn't spend some money on these things, (because to a certain extent they do provide some comfort and entertainment) and I have some of these luxuries, and to be honest, I enjoy driving a nice car, watching a big TV and playing with the gadgets, but I can afford it!

I don't borrow to spend on the luxuries, I wait till I can afford them, and I live within my means. If I can't afford it at that time, I don't buy it! Work hard, make more money, budget and save up till it is within budget, then enjoy.

Just think about the things you spend your money on. If you found yourself in a crisis how much would you get back by selling them in order to help you out of the situation?

You need to live within your means and not grow too quickly. Search out how you can make the majority of your money reproduce, then you can enjoy the rest.

This is a Godly principle, to be found faithful with the little you have, and then more will be added unto you.

I just need to throw this point in here; spending time with family is a wise use of money as well.

Quality time with friends and family doesn't have to always cost money. You can find things to do that are simple. Remember, kids don't realise how much you spend on gadgets, bills and debts, they just enjoy time with parents.

I'm not saying keep all your money and be grumpy and isolated. No, on the contrary, I am saying it is wise to pay close attention to where your money goes, and how much value you are getting from your hard earned cash.

It is He who has given you the ability to produce wealth.

The parable of the talents: Part 3
Matthew 25:14-30

Let's begin by quickly summarising the last two parts. In part one; we learned that each man was entrusted with a set amount of money according to his ability. We saw that this proves, our track record in regards to use of money up until this point determines how much more we will receive.
Part two we saw that the first two servants put their money to work and gained a one hundred percent increase on what they did with the money.
We learnt from that, we should really study where and what we spend our hard earned money for. Are we getting the best value for it, or are we just wasting it on bills, worldly pleasures, gadgets and gizmos that depreciate? Or is it working for us as hard as we work for it?

Now let's see what we can learn from the third servant's use of what he was given:

But the man who had received the one talent went off, dug a hole in the ground and hid his master's money.
Matthew 25: 18.

There are quite a few lessons to learn here, so let's start with the most important. We see that all three servants were given according to their ability. The third servant was only given one talent. This shows that no matter what our track record has been up until this point, there is still hope.

God will always give us chances to start again. Begin a new record as it were.

Maybe you have had a change of heart and character.
Maybe what you have today might be another chance for you to start over. Begin a new track record. Why not start today again, by proving you can be found trustworthy with what you have. Never despise small beginnings because this is the key to developing your ability. If you don't have very much today, be wise in your use of it and stop begging prayers for more. According to this parable, which Jesus himself is teaching, each of us is given according to what we can handle.
If you don't have very much then guess what, it is your past use of money that is limiting you. It's the choices you have made with how you spend your money that is actually keeping you there. This might sound blunt but we need to learn these things now while we still have the chance. I believe these are life changing lessons Jesus is showing us.

Another lesson is this; they were all servants of the same master, which means that this lazy servant might have even seen the other two making more on their investment. The least he could have done was to do what they were doing in order to get the same results they were getting. What would have been even smarter would have been to loan his one talent to the other guys and asked them to work it for him and make it grow. This would have taught him that he can still be lazy but get others to do the work for him and make his money grow.

But instead he hid it in the ground, remained in his comfort zone, just wanting everything to be safe and smooth sailing. No risks or work, just business as usual and predictable. He threw away his chance to step out and do something different because as we learn later, it was out of fear.

What are you afraid of? Is fear the one thing that is actually limiting you today? Are you praying for things to be different yet you are not willing to try something different? Are you hoping and praying for different results yet you are doing the same things?

It is a definition of insanity to keep doing the same think but expecting different results.

You need to make the first move in order to make change happen. Seize the opportunities in front of you today; don't let your track record with money limit your tomorrow. Step out in faith, do something different, something positive with what you have. Begin a new track record, work your ability with the little you have right now, you don't have much to lose.

It is He who has given you the ability to produce wealth.

The parable of the talents: Part 4
Matthew 25:14-30

In parts one, two and three, we learned some very important principles from the servant's perspectives. So now in part four, let's study the return of the master, his response to the servants and their rewards.

Please remember, this parable is being taught by Jesus himself. It is not a story that He heard somewhere, it is not from an ancient book or scroll, it is live and directly from the throne room of heaven.

I can't really go into detail of what a parable is in this book, but on my website www.u-can2.net, there is a study guide there entitled "what is a parable" In there we study from scripture why Jesus taught in parables.

Jesus in this parable is giving us an analogy of what the relationship between God and us is like. So in this parable (like many others) the focus is on our use of money and our ability to control it and not allow it to control us.

After a long time the master of those servants returned and settled accounts with them. The man who received the five talents brought the other five. "Master," he said, "you entrusted me with five talents. See, I have gained five more."

His master replied, "Well done, good and faithful servant! You have been faithful with a few things; I will put you in charge of many things. Come and share your master's happiness!"

Also the man who received two talents brought the other two. "Master," he said, "you entrusted me with two talents. See, I have gained two more."
His master replied, "Well done, good and faithful servant! You have been faithful with a few things; I will put you in charge of many things. Come and share your master's happiness!"
Matthew 25:19-23.

Now here is a major point of this entire book. This is where God wants you to be. Look at the master's response to both men who had increased what they were given. The King James Version of the Bible puts it this way: *I will make you ruler over much (KJV).*

The master's response was exactly the same with both the servants who had doubled what they were given. The point I want to focus on here is this; they were found faithful with a little money, notice, the master didn't give them more money. He entrusted them with power, he put them in a position of authority, made them rulers over much where they would share in the master's happiness.
What Jesus is pointing out here, is that it's not about money; money is not the end result. It's about power, control, ruling and being in a position of authority. Children of God, we really need to get this whole money mentality out of our heads before we can truly benefit from the happiness Christ has set before us. You will not receive loads of money, but in the trial process, your character will be tested through money. Your ability to rule over it; control it; reproduce it; be faithful enough to acknowledge who it comes from; have it but not rely on and put all your trust in it.

The end result, according to this parable is that if you are found faithful with little, you will be promoted to a position where you will rule, you will have the power of money, where you will no longer be dependent on the money itself.

God wants to test you with money to see if you have what it takes to be a person of ruler ship qualities, somebody in authority, a high position, controller of not only money but people as well. God wants you to have power, and according to this parable, the training ground is your ability to use your finances wisely.

Later on we will study the difference between having money, and having the power of money.

Now, let's study the response of the master towards the last servant who was given just one talent. Let us see if any of us can relate to his mentality and outlook on things.

Then the man who had received the one talent came. "Master," he said, "I knew that you are a hard man, harvesting where you did not sow and gathering where you have not scattered seed. So I was afraid and went out and hid your money in the ground. See, here is what belongs to you."

His master replied, "you wicked, lazy servant! So you knew that I harvest where I have not sown and gather where I have not scattered seed? Well then, you should have at least put my money on deposit with the bankers, so that when I returned I would have received it back with interest."

Matthew 25:24-27.

There are two points I would like us to really focus on. Number one, the master called him lazy. But why was the master referring to him as lazy, if the master gave to each man according to their ability in the first place?

Now that's a great question. The answer is that this servant was basically handed another chance to re-write his track record, he had the opportunity to be something else, try something different, do something, but yet he just did nothing as usual.

He probably just did what was expected of him. Based on his response to the master, he had a similar excuse to many of us today; fear.

Fear is what really holds most of us back. But how many times have you overcome fear in your own life? Let's use the example of learning to ride a bike. Maybe you were afraid that you might fall off. And you probably did fall.

But did you give up? Or did you get back up, keep trying to over come that fear? Eventually you have success; you learn to ride a bike. But the person who says "I will never ride a bike because I might fall" will never ride a bike. Yes you will fall off a few times, you might get a few cuts and bruises, it might even hurt a bit, but the end goal should far outweigh the problems you have at present, and yes you will make mistakes on the way, that's just life. But if your trust is completely in God, like a loving father he will be there to pick you up again. Never be afraid of making mistakes, it helps build character or backbone, there's a saying," The man who never made a mistake, never made anything" Nothing worth having in life ever comes easy, you just have to go for it and keep trying.

Keep pushing yourself; you never know what you can achieve until you try. Everything in life seems hard at first until you know how.

So fear is a good thing, it helps you build your faith in God. What you have in your hand today is an opportunity to make others change their ideas of who you are and what you're able to do.
The world today tries to strike fear in all the middle class workers, in order to keep them propping up the economy. There is a lot of negative press at the moment about how bad things are. The newspapers are selling multimillions because people who never used to buy newspapers are now buying them just to find out what is going on in the economy. But what do they know? They just sell papers.

We need to stop looking and reading all this negative press, it is scaring us into a corner where we are just hanging on to the little we have and hoping that nothing takes us by surprise.
Look what the Bible says about listening to rumours:

Whoever watches the wind will not plant; who ever looks at the cloud will not reap.
Ecclesiastes 11:4.

If you keep watching and trying to predict what is going on out there, you will be scared to death. There is too much uncertainty. But the word of God is true and steadfast.

Second point: The master said *"you should have at least put my money on deposit with the bankers, so that when I returned, I would have received it back with interest"*.

Here is something quite subtle, because if you remember, this parable was told over 2,000 years ago. Notice how the master puts the lowest emphasis on money being deposited in the bank.

In other words, the master is basically saying, the least productive use of money is to put it in the bank. So even if you were lazy, saving money in the bank is at least profitable.

But why does this parable teach us that the least use of our money is to put it in the Bank? The world today is telling us that we should put all our money in the bank as soon as we get paid.

Well let's study how banks work. They actually treat us like we are stupid, and in some cases they play on our ignorance. They make us feel like they are the ones doing us a favour by looking after our hard earned cash.

But ask yourself this question. Where do the banks get their money from to be able to loan it all over the place? It's from us!

When we put our money in the bank, we are lucky if we are getting at least three percent interest on our deposit. The bank then takes your money and lends it to your neighbour as a loan, mortgage, credit card or some other financial product, and they are making twenty to thirty percent interest, sometimes even more, on what we gave them in the first place.

Here we are so grateful for the scraps they give us from the profit they made off our money. That doesn't seem fair.

Now let me enlighten you a little on what is really happening to your money when it sits in a bank account apparently accumulating interest.

Let's say you are even lucky enough or you have searched high and low to find an interest rate of four percent, you think you're doing well. But what the banks and the elite don't tell you is that there's something called inflation. This is basically the cost of living. So the price of life's necessities like petrol, food items, clothing, TV licence, taxes, gas, electricity and so on, go up or cost more from year to year. Let's use the present day scenario when I'm writing this book: inflation is currently running at four and a half percent, so you see, with a savings rate of four percent you are already losing half a percent; your money is decreasing by half a percent. The real value of whatever you saved has already been slashed by half a percent.

So when you take your money out in a year's time, the cost of living would have gone up, so you can't buy as much with it as you would have at the start of the year. This is known as spending power. Your money's spending power decreases every year as the cost of living increases.

It is important to always take into account the true value of saved money: what you can buy today for one hundred pounds, next year would cost even more.

Please understand, I'm not talking about gadgets and gizmos, I am talking about the essentials for day to day living, food, clothing, heating etc.

So is the Bible saying then we should not put any money in the bank? No! That is not smart; it is good to have money put aside for a rainy day in-case the unfortunate happens.   But it is saying, having money in the bank should not be your priority.

Be wise when looking for a savings account, we need to be educated because there is something else in this country England that affects our savings.   It is tax on the interest you make on your money. This is twenty percent.   So even when your savings goes up by four percent, the government taxes out of that four percent increase, twenty percent.   So let's visualise it, let's say you begin with ten thousand pounds:

| You invest £10,000 at 4% in your local bank | You earn £400 in interest for the year | But you pay £80 in tax on that interest at 20% | So your net earnings are £320, resulting in a balance of £10,320 |

$$£10,000 + £400 - £80 = £10,320$$

But take a hypothetical inflation rate of 3.5% and see what happens to your 'buying power'

$$£10,320 - 3.5\% (£361.20) = £9,958.80$$

At the end of the year, you are actually **£41.20** worst off.   Your spending power is less than when you started.

So when it comes to saving your money, you need to find a way of saving that is not taxed. There is currently a tax free saving account called an ISA (Individual Savings Account). You then need to find out how much inflation is currently running at and get a savings account that either tracks inflation or is running above the rate of inflation, and then finally you need to find an account that offers compound interest, which is a way of your interest accumulating.

Compound interest basically means receiving interest on the interest you have earned. The banks already do this with the money you owe on a credit card. If you do not repay each month in full, you get charged a set amount of interest. This is added to the amount you owe and interest is charged on the new figure. So they keep charging interest on top of interest. That's why your debt seems to grow so quickly.

If you can find a savings account that offers compound interest as well as tax free, as well as inflation tracking! that will be a good account to go for. So normally when you save money in the bank, they only give you interest on what you initially deposited. So if you started off with one hundred pounds and the rate was four percent, your interest would be four pounds at the end of the year, but they won't add that four pounds to next years, so instead of you getting interest on one hundred and four pounds, they will only give you another four pounds because the interest is not compounded. You are only earning four percent on your initial one hundred pounds deposit.

I hope now you can understand why the Bible, which was written over two thousand years ago, put such a low priority on your money being deposited in the bank. It says the least use of your money is to put it in the bank.

So use your time wisely when it comes to your hard-earned money, you deserve to make it work for you.

Here's my last point while we are bashing the banking system. It can fail! Which it has done in 2008. If you have truly understood what I have just explained, you are a little bit wiser and intend to take the advice of finding a savings account or scheme that is tax free, offers an inflation-beating rate of return and offers compound interest. You will then be doing something smarter with your money than you have in the past. You want to make your money work as hard for you as you do for it. You want to do something different, but to find a saving scheme that offers all these benefits take time. So now you can appreciate the saying "time is money" because the more time you spend researching savings options, the more money you will make in the long run.

So don't be lazy with your hard earned cash anymore. Don't just deposit it in the first account you see. Do something different, save it wisely, this is a Biblical principle that will yield much more than taking the bank's word for it. Why work hard for your money then just give it away to someone else to profit from it?

Now also you can see how much effort it is going to require in order to find an effective way of saving money, you can see that this scripture is teaching us that it is better to spend more time trying to make money than it is trying to save it.

I come across so many people who go through so much effort trying to cut corners, sell things, eat less and all these other money saving schemes. But I say to them, if you put this much effort into actually making more money as you do trying to save it, you will be better off.

Use your skill, your God-given talent, work smarter instead of harder. We need to prioritise, because I tell you, the government is always coming up with new ways to squeeze the innocent, in order to pay for what the guilty have stolen.

It is He who has given you the ability to produce wealth.

The parable of the talents: Part 5
Matthew 25:14-30

From part four, we learnt about taking time to invest our money wisely, if you do this you then you understand that time is money. So let's see how it works Biblically.

The parable states in verse *16-17: The man who had received five talents went at once and put his money to work and gained five more. So also, the one with the two talents gained two more.*

The point we will build on is this. Both servants went out immediately. Please understand something here, I'm not saying you should just go out today with your entire pay, and put it all to work somehow and then expect to gain a massive return, and then you will have great success, No! There is a very important principle here. These two servants were still in the employment of the master, the money they used, was what they had extra, on top of what they would normally get. This was money given to them unexpectedly.

What do you do with unexpected money? Do you use it to pay back your debts, or do you work it straight away? These two servants knew the importance of time. Time is one of the few things in life that you can never get back. It is constantly going by.

I have a great motivational trick I use when teaching people about Biblical economics. I get a normal clock or watch which has the three hands, hour, minute and second.

We sit down and just watch as the seconds hand goes round. Tick tock, tick tock, tick tock.
(I would advise you try this). After about a minute or two, I get them to tell me what they notice from the exercise. If you do this for yourself, what you should notice is that no matter who you are, how nice a person, how smart, young, old, intelligent, rich, poor, Christian, non believer, successful, educated or illiterate, the time just keeps going by. It doesn't care what you're doing and it doesn't wait while you learn this principle. It is no respecter of person. That's your life just ticking by. What are you doing with your time? How valuable is it to you? Don't you realise yet that you are running out of time? One of the things the older generation will teach you is that time goes by a lot quicker than you can ever imagine.

Are you the kind of person who is always putting everything off till tomorrow? Are you wondering why you seem to be poor all the time, always in debt? Why your finances never seem to get any better? You just seem to be going round in circles each month. Well it has a lot to do with how you spend and value your time.

Go to the ant, you sluggard; consider its ways and be wise! It has no commander, no overseer or ruler, yet it stores its provisions in summer and gathers its food at harvest.
Proverbs 6:6-8.

From this passage, you notice that the ants are always planning ahead. I hear this all the time, people saying I want to work for myself, be my own boss. I want to start my own business and so on and so forth, but they are doing the same thing with their time.

Those who feel they are really serious, when they come home from work, watch those programmes like dragons den, and the apprentice, get themselves all fired up and motivated for a moment, then they realise that they have work in the morning so they got to go bed. "Yeah we start in the morning, tomorrow"
The Bible teaches against that:

How long will you lie there, you sluggard? When will you get up from your sleep? A little sleep, a little slumber, a little folding of the hands to rest and poverty will come on you like a bandit and scarcity like an armed man.
Proverbs 6:9-11.

Man you need to stay up and get going, time is passing you by, wise is always to start earlier.
So now let me expose something to you about the human mind. Companies spend millions on psychologists in order of finding ways to more effectively use their employees; how can we get the best use of our staff? So these psychologists go out and do surveys on people and also the human mind, in order to find out how it works, what makes us very productive, and what makes us dull.

I found out from their research, that the human mind can actually be split into three time frames.
An A time,
B time and
C time.

The A time is when you are at your most productive, your mind is working effortlessly coming up with ideas and solutions, being creative and extremely logical. Your peak.

The B time is when your mind is just still a bit productive but not as efficient, kind of like overdrive or auto pilot, just going on the path of what you set it on during you're A time.

The C time is basically shut down, relax and process time, where what you have done during the A and B time is now being evaluated; your mind is starting to shut down, getting ready for rest. With some people, this is overloaded during the first two time frames.

Now most companies who pay a lot of money for learning how to make better use of their employees all know this, so they use this principle against us in order to keep us on the same level. You see your A time is the first three to four hours from when you just wake up after having a good night's sleep. During this time the course of your entire day is set. For most people this is when you are at your peak, at your best mentally, you are most productive; all your mental powers are working at their highest capacity. Man you're on fire and you can do anything.

Just think on this, what are you doing with that time? Most of us use it to get ready, rush around with the kids, and then give the rest to our jobs.

Let me tell you, if you really want to make something better of yourself, start earlier, use some of your A time for you. Use it on your ambitions. Instead of waking up, hitting the snooze button a few times then rushing to work, why not wake up a little earlier? You won't get anywhere if you keep wasting your A time, if you just give it all to your work but yet you want to do something for yourself. Even if you do achieve something, it takes a lot of unnecessary hard work if you don't do it in your prime or make better use of your A time.

How much further in life would you be today if you had started earlier?

Don't you know the saying? "The early bird catches the worm."

Also one last but very important point about your A time, this is when you set up your day. You set your emotions and attitude for the rest of the day during your A time. Notice that if you have a positive attitude when you get up, your entire day follows that positivism.

But if you wake up and your morning begins in a negative way, the rest of the day will follow that pattern.

I heard it said that your morning is like setting your thermostat at home. How will you set yours? Will you be an over comer according to the word of God? Or tired, stressed and defeated according to the lies of the enemy.

You can not pick what happens to you during your day, but you can determine how you respond to it.

Your B time is the next four hours. If you notice the pattern a normal working day follows, they use your peak time to set the day's agenda, when you're getting into overdrive, they let you have a little lunch so that you are rested and revived, then they use your B time also. Your mind is now just going on auto pilot at this point, you are settled in, you know what's happening and you are just going with the flow of the day. You are set.

Now look at your C time. This frame is basically the processing time where your mind is occupied with what has happened during the day. It's going all through it in your subconscious, storing and deleting as necessary.

Sad to say but I come across so many people who have great visions, ideas, and motives for the Kingdom of God, yet the time they try to use to achieve or explore these goals is their C time. When they get home from work, their mind is processing what happened, they realise they don't like working anymore so they have to do something.

They then try to put their mind into gear again to come up with something good but it's harder work, so they go to sleep after trying to push themselves in the C time but end up wearing themselves out even more.

So they just end up settling for "oh well, everyone else is just as miserable with their work as I am. So why bother, it will all work out one day".

If you can identify as one of these I am referring to, then maybe this is the time for you to start applying some of these principles outlined in this book.
Please don't try to do it in your C time, you really need to make better use of your A time or even your B time, then let your body and mind rest and recuperate during its C time. Apply wisdom to your thinking and achieve what ever you need to for your future.

You need to let your mind rest during your C time, try not to push yourself too much at this point, because it will affect your ability the next day. I know it means you will have to wake up earlier and try to prioritise your time. You need to manage your time better, have a plan for the day, then work through it logically, it will definitely be hard work, but trust me, I promise you will get all the rest you need in the grave!

The parable of the shrewd manager.

Luke 16:1-13

Jesus told his disciples: "There was a rich man whose manager was accused of wasting his possessions. So he called him in and asked him, what is this I hear about you? Give an account of your management, because you cannot be manager any longer."

"I know what I'll do so that, when I lose my job here, people will welcome me into their houses." So he called in each one of his masters debtors. He asked the first, "How much do you owe my master?" "Eight hundred gallons of olive oil" he replied. The manager told him, "Take your bill, sit down quickly, and make it four hundred." Then he asked the second, "And how much do you owe?" "A thousand bushels of wheat," he replied. He told him, "Take your bill and make it eight hundred."

The master commended the dishonest manager because he had acted shrewdly. For the people of this world are more shrewd with dealing with their own kind than are the people of light. I tell you, use worldly wealth to gain friends for yourselves, so that when it is gone, you will be welcomed into eternal dwellings.
"Who ever can be trusted with very little, can also be trusted with much, and whoever is dishonest with very little, will also be dishonest with much. So if you have not been trustworthy in handling worldly wealth, who will trust you with true riches? And if you have not been trustworthy with some one else's property, who will trust you with property of your own? No servant can serve two masters. Either he will hate the one and love the other, or he will be devoted to one and despise the other. You can not serve both God and money."
It is He who has given you the ability to produce wealth.

The parable of the shrewd manager. part1

What are you relying on?
Luke 16: 1-2

In this book we are learning about applying Biblical principles to our finances and everyday walk with God, in order to bring ourselves into alignment with His promise according to **Deuteronomy 8:18.** We understand that God will not release great wealth to just anyone who asks for it, but to those that do it right; according to his covenant. So this parable here, once again is being taught by Jesus himself, to help us understand the importance of how we view, use and work for money. Now it is said that this is the most confusing parable Jesus ever taught. If viewed without the interpretation of the Holy Spirit, it points to the fact that God commends a person for stealing!

But this isn't the case! There are many principles the manager finally discovered, and that is what Jesus was really pointing to. So let's take our time and go through the entire parable step by step so that we can learn and put into practice what this manager finally understood about money and most importantly how we work for it.

Jesus told his disciples: "There was a rich man whose manager was accused of wasting his possessions. So he called him in and asked him, what is this I hear about you? Give an account of your management, because you cannot be manager any longer."
Luke 16: 1-2.

The owner has been informed that this manager was being unfaithful in using the owner's money. The owner asks the manager to give an account of his use of the money.

Here is a small but very important point! If you are in employment, and are being unfaithful, or, as in this case, stealing, you will always get found out. Things can only go that way for so long, theft can only be covered up for a period of time. One day, it will be exposed. Please believe me in that. A lot of the time, when we work somewhere, we always have the tendency to believe that we are entitled to some freebies. That's not good thinking. If you are taking things without permission or knowledge of your boss, that is stealing. No matter what it is, how big or small. Taking something small like pens, stamps, stationery, or what ever it is, begins to develop a character within you. The more you get away with the little things, the more confident you become and you move on to bigger things. Your character is being changed gradually without you even realising it. I used to be like that when growing up in London. I would steal little things from work like tools, screwdrivers and so on. Then moved on to sweets from shops, chocolate, alcohol; to clothes and so on. I didn't even realise I was becoming a criminal until the day I got caught. It was embarrassing because I didn't want that. If you were to confront any law breaker within the prison system and ask how they got to that state, they will all tell you the same thing, it started unintentionally. And over time, they began believing if they wanted something, you didn't really need to work to get it, you just steal it.

I know this might sound drastic and over the top; you might be saying that won't happen to me, its just a few pens and sticky pads or whatever it is I'm taking home. But my point is this; over time you will get caught out, you might even loose your job. Now is that really worth it? You see you can't justify theft, no matter how big or small to the person you are stealing from.

Your employer will not judge you by anything else but by what you have been found out to do. Their trust is gone. Now that is actually just a small point. Stealing actually says to God that He can't really provide for you. You are basically saying that He doesn't take care of you and you can't fully trust Him to supply all your needs. God will not bless or release wealth into the life of a lawbreaker. Or to a person who is not completely committed and trusting in Him. You are unusable if you can't be found faithful enough to trust God for everything. So for your own good, if you're doing that, and not being faithful with someone else's money, or property, you need to stop!

Point number two, from the outset, this parable indicates that money does not belong to us. Money is the most sensitive subject in the entire body of Christ; when you start talking about money people begin to get uncomfortable, they start getting edgy and squirming in their seats, they wish you would just move on and talk about something else. The reason is; they love it! They covet it and recognise its power more easily than anything else. All they care about is that it's theirs. They have worked for it, it's their reward and they want to keep and hold onto it dearly.

But in the Kingdom of God it is completely different. You have to view money as a tool; something you don't hold onto but you use for an end result. You know a tool does not really hold any true value; it is your use of that tool which produces something. It is your use of money that holds the true value. If I had one hundred pounds, in one instance I bought some gold with it, (which is actually going up in value) and in another instance I spent it all on a night out getting drunk and throwing up everywhere. Which would you say had more value? Maybe I had a great time on my night out. I forgot all about it though, but it was fun; I think.

You see, it is the same amount of money used in each instance but one has a long term value, while the other, I don't even remember. What you use your money for, actually values it. Until we can detach ourselves from the love of money, we will always need it, and we won't be using it in the right way.

Third point: Immediately the manager is asked to give an account of his stewardship, he begins to panic.

In your life today, if God was to ask you to give an account of your use of money, what would your reaction be? Would you panic like this manager here? Are you comfortable with the way you use money?
If not, then now is a perfect time to change your view and use of money. There is still hope for you!

We should not be selfishly motivated with our use of money. It should not be all me, me, me; I've got to take care of my needs first, I need to pay my bills, I have to feed my family; when I'm rich and taken care of, then I will begin to think about the needs of the church and the work here on earth of spreading the gospel. If you can get beyond wanting, needing and spending all your money on your needs, God can begin to use you; He can release more finances into your household because he knows that you will use it wisely and not just hoard it all for your needs.

One day you too will be asked to give an account of your use of money, because God is looking for those He can entrust with wealth in order to establish His covenant and meet the needs of a hurting world. So today, why not begin to use money as a tool; entrusted to you by God, to make a difference in this world.

These are the five things God has entrusted us with:

1. LIFE. What you received. You don't own it, it was purchased by Jesus.
2. TIME. What you have been allotted. We have a set amount of time on earth. No one knows when it will be over.
3. TALENTS. What you have been given for your use.
4. POSESSIONS. What you have been entrusted with.
5. FINANCE. What you have laboured for. How have you been spending your money? You don't go to work because you are a nice person.

We will have to give an account for these one day. These are things we do not own. God is the giver, possessor, owner and rewarded.

Man is the receiver, a steward, responsible and accountable to God. God has entrusted these things to our control for the use and benefit of advancing His Kingdom. We are the ambassadors and administrators of the Kingdom here on earth.

Let's walk like royalty!

It is He who has given you the ability to produce wealth.

The parable of the shrewd manager. Part2

What are you relying on?
Luke 16: 3-4

The manager has now been told that he will be losing his job! Panic really sets in.

The manager said to himself, "what shall I do now? My master is taking away my job. I'm not strong enough to dig, and I'm ashamed to beg. I know what I'll do so that when I lose my job here, people will welcome me into their homes."
Luke 16:3-4.

Straight away from this reaction, it is clear that, though he has been stealing money from his master, he has been spending it unwisely. How do we know this? Because he obviously had nothing of real value to show for it. He was probably spending the extra money he was getting on vain living, material things and just squandering it away on things which have no long term value. If this was not the case he wouldn't have reacted in this way.

Now ask yourself, what are you spending your money on? Is there any long-term value in the things you own? What is the resale value? Are you working hard for your money, and then just spending most of it on little pockets of pleasure every weekend? trying to find release in worldly pleasures?

I come across people who sell things of value like precious metals, Gold, Silver, metal extracts (which are going up in value) to buy things which are going down in value, like mobile phones, handbags, widescreen TVs, play stations, mobile phones, cars and so on. That is absolutely ridiculous.

They have an incorrect mentality, spending money on things they don't need but just really want because the world has advertised them so expertly and told us that our lives will be empty without these things. I know people in high powered, high paying jobs, who during the week work hard, then at the weekend just squander it in the pubs, clubs and bars, getting drunk, then doing it all over again the following week. Earning money but living a very empty life. Let me tell you two things, firstly, money does not guarantee you happiness. Secondly, God will not release wealth into stupidity. God does not bless our ignorance.

You need to have something of value to show for your use of money. No matter where your money comes from, use it wisely, put it in something that goes up in value so in the time of crisis, (and believe me you will have a crisis so just relax about that now,) you will have something valuable to fall back on. You will have something you can sell to help you get through the situation. Some of us don't even realise what we are actually spending our money on until our eyes are opened by a time of crisis. We then see reality and how material things can only give us pleasure; but can't help us out of a tight situation or through a rainy day.

Please understand, I am not condemning these worldly things, I'm not saying you shouldn't buy nice cars, big screen TVs, fancy watches, posh phones, handbags. I'm not saying you shouldn't go out with your friends and family to have a good time socialising, because I have and also do all these things too. To a certain extent, I enjoy them, its fun. The luxuries of life are nice. But I have and do these things when I can afford them. I don't put too high a priority on it. Unhappily there are people who would rather stop giving to support a church than cancel their sky subscription, or lose any other worldly pleasure, when times get hard.

Statistics have shown that the majority of people, in times of crisis, start by cutting back on their giving; whether it is to charity or a local church. But it should be the other way round, start by releasing yourself from worldly bondages and contracts.

Evaluate where you are spending just to please your own desires. Try to cut back on those things that tie you in for a long time like, expensive phone contracts; TV subscriptions, Gym memberships and such. In a crisis, you need to travel light, there is no point having unnecessary baggage dragging you down and taking up space in your head. Find value in the things of the Kingdom of God. Put your money in things that have true value.

It is He who has given you the ability to produce wealth.

The parable of the shrewd manager. Part3

What are you relying on?
Luke 16: 4-7

Now in this part we see that this manager begins to really panic about his future. Reality has finally hit him, he can no longer rely on what he had always assumed would be there for him. He is no longer operating on the auto pilot that was guiding him when there was a regular work routine. He is now in survival mode. Look what the manager did when he realised it was coming to an end. He used money to affect his future.

"I know what I'll do so that, when I lose my job here, people will welcome me into their houses." So he called in each one of his master's debtors. He asked the first, "How much do you owe my master?" "Eight hundred gallons of olive oil" he replied. The manager told him, "Take your bill, sit down quickly, and make it four hundred." Then he asked the second, "And how much do you owe?" "A thousand bushels of wheat," he replied. He told him, "Take your bill and make it eight hundred."
Luke 16: 4-7.

So from this part, we learn that losing your job will make you think quickly on your feet. Reality has set in, he needs a solution, he doesn't just start crying and praying and wondering what will happen to him in the future. No, he begins to work on a plan.

Today you need to ask yourself certain questions, are you going through life just floating along with no plans for the future? No real goals or dreams? Are you just relying on your job to always be there to provide for you?

This parable is teaching us an important lesson. If you found out tomorrow that you were going to be made redundant what would you do? Honestly, check your life to answer this question; do you have a backup plan? Have you put aside anything for such a crisis? Do you own anything of real value that you could sell to help you through this time of transition? Or is all the money you have been earning up till now just been spent on servicing your debts, monthly bills and worldly desires?

You know, we need to be thinking about this while we have the chance, while we are still able to do something about it! Your future needs to be in your present, you can't only just rely on your job being there for you for ever.

Now to those of you who are smart enough, that when I asked the question about losing your job, you did not panic because you have certain things in place; certain ideas already in the pipeline, that you know what you would do immediately. It would actually be a blessing to be made redundant at this point because you can then focus on your ideas.

Let me ask you this question, why wait?

Why do we always wait till a crisis before we dig deep and discover our inner talent? The majority of the owners of real global companies, entrepreneurs, directors, inventors and so on, if you were to ask them how they started up, you would find the same answers. Most ceo's started because they were forced to do something in order to survive. Most started because they lost their jobs and couldn't find work, so they needed to do something, anything, just to survive. They then discovered an inner survival mode, which was only exposed in a time of crisis.

The crisis pulled out all their resources, and they discovered a talent inside of them, which they had never needed to use before.

You will find that not one of them ever regrets losing their jobs because they will all tell you that it was the best thing that ever happened to them.

You know, when you are at rock bottom, there is no where else to go but up!
A loser gives up, throws in the towel and stays defeated. But a winner pulls himself up and finds a way to survive. It is the easiest thing in the world to give up, but it's the hardest thing in the world to pick yourself up and keep going.

Are you relying on your job to always provide for you? A lot of the time, our jobs can be one of the biggest hindrances to our financial goals. The routine of just working then getting paid can lure you into a false sense of security. It creates a comfort zone that we just get used to. We think it will always be there for us, so we buy things on credit based on the fact that we will always receive a set income to service those debts. That is dangerous, very high risk.

So today I encourage you to begin thinking about your future. How do you use what you earn regularly, what are your long term or backup plans? What are you working for? Are you just relying on your job for your security?

You never know what you can really achieve until you take the first step.

It won't be easy, but let me assure you of this, relying on your natural, God-given talent is a lot safer and more rewarding than any job can ever offer you.

Sow your seed in the morning, and at evening let not your hands be idle, for you do not know which will succeed, whether this or that or whether both will do equally well.
Ecclesiastes 11:6.

Sowing the seed is a type of work. It is basically saying, do your work when it needs to be done, during your working day, then when you finish work (in the evening or whenever it is) do not be idle. In other words, don't just rely on your job; don't let your hands be idle. Referring to the hands means what you have, your God-given talent. Do something with it because you don't know what will succeed. Maybe even both will succeed.

So don't be lazy, have a plan, put it into action and watch which will have lasting value.

It is He who has given you the ability to produce wealth.

The parable of the shrewd manager. Part4

What are you relying on?
Luke 16: 8-9

Now up till this point, the manager had been stealing money, but obviously doing nothing with it which holds true value. Put yourself in his position: up till this point, you have just been working and relying on your consistent income to provide for you, what would you do if it came to an end? In this crisis, this manager learnt something more valuable than money itself. He understood that what he did today with money, can actually secure his tomorrow. He realised finally that the wise use of money, whether it was his or not, can take care of his needs in the future. Now he was being commended for acting shrewdly.

The master commended the dishonest manager because he had acted shrewdly. For the people of this world are more shrewd with dealing with their own kind than are the people of light. I tell you, use worldly wealth to gain friends for yourselves, so that when it is gone, you will be welcomed into eternal dwellings.
Luke 16: 8-9.

This parable, (remember it is being told by Jesus himself) is very confusing because it looks here that because his master commended him, and said well done, that was smart, people believe this means that he was commended for stealing! That's not the case.

The real lesson here is that, if you act wisely with planning for your future, you will be commended for it. The manager acted wisely when he was in the midst of a crisis.

This shows that there is still a chance for you to change your outlook on things. Things aren't as bad as they seem.

Then the Lord said to Cain, "Why are you angry? Why is your face downcast? If you do what is right, will you not be accepted? But if you do not do what is right, sin is crouching at your door; it desires to have you, but you must master it."
Genesis 4: 6-7.

Here God said to Cain, if you do well, I will accept you. So for us, there is still hope, we can do well and be accepted, If you do good, you will get a 'well done', if you are smart with your money, you will reap a harvest.

The manager was not commended for his stealing, infact; he lost his job for stealing! But he was being commended for the future plans he had made for himself when he would be un-employed. He finally understood the true value of money, and how to use it wisely. Notice, he stopped stealing and keeping it for himself, but he helped others with it. Your use of money today can affect your future in a positive or negative way. When you give to a church, the money is used to keep the ministry going, keep the doors open and the good news of Jesus Christ being shared.

In that instance, it's not just your future which is being affected, but the lives of others are being transformed. You are now not being selfish in your use of money and saying, "this is my money, I worked hard for it" but you are now using it to help others. The second half of this portion states that unbelievers are shrewder in dealing with their own kind than Christians. Worldly wealth can be used to gain friends; so that when it is no longer here, there would be people we helped along the way to support us.

If you want to use money wisely and be commended for it, then according to this parable, you need to stop being selfish with it.

Money is just a tool. You should use it to build your future; giving to a church is the same as sending your money to heaven. There is a heavenly account which I have already shown you earlier in this book, (supporting God's prophets) that will prove the case of a heavenly account where you can send your money ahead of you.

One last point I would like us to notice here, is that the master was so detached from his money, that even when someone was stealing from him, he didn't worry or cry or even get mad. He actually commended this person that was stealing his money.

Man that is a great picture. To be mature enough to understand, that your money is not what holds true value, but it is your ability to produce it that is valuable.

Don't you know, you are it! You are the one that produces wealth, the work you do, the skills you have, the education you have received, that is what actually pays your bills. I have heard of so many wealthy people who have lost it all, been at rock bottom after living in such abundance, but still somehow manage to get it all back again within a short period of time. People ask them, how did you do it after losing everything? They always say, "Yes I did lose all my money, but I did not lose my mind." It is what you can do with your skills and talents that actually gain you the success. This master here knew that even though his manager was stealing from him, he could always make the money back. He didn't rely on the stuff for his security; he relied on his skill to produce more things.

You hear stories of very successful men and women who at one point in their life lost it all. I mean down to their last penny, but yet in just a short space of time, they manage to gain it all back. People always are amazed by this. If you then ask the individual how they did it, you would get the same response. Yes they lost it all, but they did not loose their mind. Their ability to make it back was always within them. They just started again. Don't let your worldly possessions be your security, or define you. You are it!

Are you detached from your worldly possessions that if someone stole from you, you could act in the same manner?

You would just think, "Oh well, maybe they needed it more than I do." Or do you rely just on your worldly possessions to make you who you are? Do you rely on your money for security?

Today, begin to work on your natural ability, your gifting, the thing that you do well with the least effort, whatever it is.

What are you really good at?

Try to be good at one thing, then practice continually till you are the best at it.
Then you can start relying on your God-given talent and ability to sustain you, rather than a job you probably don't even like. Be the best you you can be.

It is He who has given you the ability to produce wealth.

The parable of the shrewd manager. Part5

What are you relying on?
Luke 16: 10-13

"Who ever can be trusted with very little, can also be trusted with much, and whoever is dishonest with very little, will also be dishonest with much. So if you have not been trustworthy in handling worldly wealth, who will trust you with true riches? And if you have not been trustworthy with some one else's property, who will trust you with property of your own? No servant can serve two masters. Either he will hate the one and love the other, or he will be devoted to one and despise the other. You can not serve both God and money."
Luke 16: 10-13.

So as we come to the end of this parable being taught by Jesus, we learn why this dishonest manager was being commended; it was because he finally understood the use of money. He now realised the true value of money, and how it could be used wisely in planning for his future.
A lot of the time, we only think about the here and now when it comes to the use of our money. We make decisions based on impulse, we go with our emotions over sound judgement, and then later on wonder why we don't ever seem to have enough leftover. Some people say, "I have too much month left at the end of my money."

There is something I learned, which I call "a moment". Companies or organisations need to capture you in that moment, in order to sell you something. In that moment, your mind can go completely blank and all you see is just what they are trying to sell to you.

When I figured this out, I then began to train myself in how to get round this: overcome the moment. I would walk away for a while, try to detach emotions from my decision and really think about how spending that money would affect my future. Then I make a decision out of my own motivation rather than people pushing things on me. You should try this for yourself if you really want to make a change in your life. If you want to change how you view money, if you really want to prove to God that you are faithful with what you have in your hands, you need to have people with whom you can talk when it comes to making a financial decision. Think of two or three people whose judgement you trust, who are quite good with money. When you want to make a purchase, you can just give them a call and ask their opinion. I'm not talking about small financial decisions like petrol, or essential things, I mean like mobile phone contracts, TVs, mortgages, bank accounts, loans, credit cards, what ever financial decision, even the use of your income. You know this is about being honest with what you have, be straight with your friends, try to surround yourself or keep good friends with whom you can actually share your financial problems and decisions with.

When I started doing this, they helped me out of a lot of situations because they knew my financial status, and when I was getting caught out in a moment of madness, I would always be talked around it. Changed my life!

This was great because it worked for a while, but then when I found this hard to do; my next step was to open a separate account. Then whenever I almost made an impulse purchase (no matter how big or small, from chocolate bars to a new TV) of something I didn't really need, the money I would have spent then, I would put it into the account so it would be like I had spent the money anyway. My intention for that money, was when I had built it up a bit, I would treat myself from time to time on something I really wanted.

Nothing wrong with that, I would have spent it anyway; but what used to then happen was instead of me spending that money I had accumulated, the money would always be used to get me out of a tight spot. Whenever we were just about to run out of money, have no petrol in the car or had no food left in the house, that money was always there to help us out at that moment.

This taught me a huge lesson (which I enjoy teaching others) that if I had made all those impulse buys at the moment they arose, we would be in an unnecessary financial difficulty which those things I would have spent the money on, would never have been able to help us out of.

Man that was an awesome lesson.

I advise you to begin to think, how am I spending my money? How are my financial decisions affecting my future? Am I putting more value on material things which depreciate, than making sound financial decisions? What are my friends like, and can I ask them for advise on things, or will they just always think of me as either being poor, or being too rich and rubbing it in their faces?

You work hard for your money, so it makes no sense just squandering it on impulse purchases.
This also says that who ever can be trusted with very little, can also be trusted with much. Here is a great principle because this is what this entire book is about, your character; what type of person are you, and how do you view money?
Are you some one that money has a tight grip on? Are you a stingy person? Selfish? Vain? Only after what God can do for you? Are you a lover of money and the power it has? These are characteristics of a person who is un-useable.
In-order to receive the true riches of heaven, you will be first tested with a little, before you can be trusted with much.

This also states that people of this world are smarter with dealing with their own kind, than the children of God. This is a very true statement because as believers, we tend to talk and hope that faith will walk the walk for us.

That's impossible! We live in a worldly system, so we need to operate according to that system. You can't go to the supermarket and by faith pay for your shopping!

You can't go t the petrol station, prophecy over the cashier, bring them a word from God, and they give you your petrol for free! NO! We have to operate within the laws of this world. So we need to be wise and use worldly things as a tool in order to secure our future.

If you have been dishonest with little, you will be dishonest with much. Here again, our character is being questioned. You will be tested with little. People say I can't give because I don't have much. That's perfect, because that is where you are actually being tested, what are you doing with the little you have? There is no use praying for more money because you will just do the same with it. There is still a chance that you can be a giver even with the little you have now; you can still prove to God that he can get money through you to a hurting, needy world.

Now here's the big one, no servant can serve two masters. You cannot serve God and money. That is a very strong statement there. It is asking you a question that you really need to take your time thinking about it before you answer.

Why do you get up in the morning? Why do you go to work? Why do you do whatever it is you do? Is it for the Kingdom of Heaven, or is it just so that you can service your bills and keep a roof over your head? Are you forced to work because you need to fill your life with material things?

You cannot serve God if you are a servant of money, if you place a higher priority on worldly things and worldly get together than you do on church functions, then you need to check if you are right with God.

When God release his abundance into your life, it will not be because he loves you more than anyone else, it will be for the purpose and benefit of his kingdom. You will be a vessel through which he can get his finances through to a world desperate for the good news of Jesus Christ. It will be to prove that man can not live by bread alone, but according to the word of God, "by the word of God".

So decide in your heart, to seek first the kingdom.

But seek first his Kingdom and his righteousness, and all these things shall be added unto you.
Matthew 6:33.

The word there "added" means on top of what you already have, not just for your family, but for the world that are in need. It will only go to those who seek to put in the work for the Kingdom of Heaven first.

So choose for yourself today, who are you willing to serve?

In order to establish His covenant on the earth.

The ways versus the acts of God.

Psalm 119:97-100

As we go into this last section of the book, looking into the covenant God has already set before us, we will be bringing the entire teaching on why God wants us wealthy to a close. The final evidence; It is to establish His covenant. Throughout **Deuteronomy 8:18**, we see the word referring to God as HE, used three times in that one verse. This is a definite conviction that it is God's will for us to be living in a life of abundance, a life flowing with His continual provision. But it doesn't happen overnight. To enter and receive this covenant operating in your life, you need to understand and walk according to the ways of God. This covenant will only be between God and those who choose to do it right, in obedience with every word that is written. Gods ways are life changing and sustainable.

First let us begin by defining the word covenant. In the dictionary it is explained as;
A binding agreement
A formal sealed agreement or contract
A signed written agreement between two or more parties to perform some actions.
An agreement between God and His people in which God makes certain promises and requires certain behaviour from them in return.

To live in Gods covenant means to be found faithful in obedience to His word. We have to learn and be directed by the teachings in the Bible which actually train us from the inside out. To operate in covenant with God, we need to live by His ways in order to access the blessings.

Now as we study the Bible, we see that God operates in two ways: 1) His ways. 2) His acts. Here is the difference between the two. The acts of God are instant! These acts or miracles which in most cases take care of an immediate need, there and then.   Like the parting of the red sea, feeding the five thousand, and other miracles performed either by God through His prophets, or by Jesus with the power of God, down to the disciples. They are quick and absolute proof to the power and authority of God. They are to bring you into an acknowledgement of and believing in God. But the ways of God are totally different.   They are character building. It is how you think; perform; operate; the way of God should become what defines you, who you are, they take time to learn, study and rely on. They are basically sustaining principles, to take care of not just the present need, but also the future needs.

The way of God is like this; there is a Chinese proverb which says: Give a man a fish and you feed him for a day. Teach a man to fish and you feed him for a lifetime.
It is good to be given something, but if you learn how to get the thing, you will no longer rely on that one fish, you can now go off on your own, and catch your fish as and when you need it.

Which is better for you? Being constantly given fish, or having the ability to catch fish? Which do you think God wants for you? To just give you one fish and feed you for today, or to teach you how to catch it for yourself? You see, when you get the thing, you will use it and need it again. It comes quickly and goes just as quickly. But if you will take the time to learn the way of how to get the thing, it will be a longer process, but you will no longer need the thing, because you will know how to get it whenever. That is the way of God. To bring you into a point of understanding that you can fend for yourself as long as you are rooted in His word.

Gods' ways are set for a reason, if you learn and obey them, they will work for you always. Wherever you are. It's like gravity. The principle remains the same all over the world. Just take a look at this passage:

Oh, how I love your law! I meditate on it all day long. Your commands make me wiser than my enemies, for they are ever with me. I have more insight than all my teachers, for I meditate on your statutes. I have more understanding than the elders, for I obey your precepts.
Psalm 119: 97-100.

This scripture teaches us that if we will study the ways of God, we will be wiser than any teacher that we would ever come across. This just speaks volumes to me, the word of God will teach you everything you need to know, and if you follow them, they will sustain you in a life of fullness according to Christ's order.

When God sets a law, it is not just in order to bring us into alignment with his will; it is also to show us his character. So in other words, you can actually flip them round on Him. That actually scared me to write it, but I pray you understand with this example. Here is a way of God that we can will flip around and see what it exposes about God:

Whoever can be trusted with very little can also be trusted with much, and whoever is dishonest with very little will also be dishonest with much.
Luke 16: 10.

Now according to this order, who ever can be trusted with little can be trusted with much, so if we flip this order around on God, He is putting it this way;

If you can not trust God with something as little as your money, your everyday provision, then what makes you think you can really trust Him with much, like your eternal life?

If you can not trust the God of the Bible with your money; in your subconscious, what makes you think you can trust him with the big things like healing, your salvation, forgiveness of your sins; past, present and future? The same God that said whatever it is you are believing for, is the same that says "Bring your tithes and offerings into my house" It is the same God through out the Bible! He is unchangeable.

In order for you to reap the benefits of his covenant, you need to be steadfast in your belief; you need an absolute trust in all is ways and laws.

You can't just pick out the ones that are easy and suit you, no! God wants all or nothing. He blesses the righteous, those who do it according to His word.

So when you learn and apply His ways into your everyday lifestyle, you will then be entitled to receive and walk in His covenant.

Therefore I tell you, do not worry about your life, what you will eat or drink; or about your body, what you will wear. Is not life more important than food, and the body more important than clothes? Look at the birds of the air; they do not sow or reap or store away in barns, and yet your Heavenly Father feeds them. Are you not more valuable than they? Who of you by worrying can add a single hour to his life? And why do you worry about clothes? See hoe the lilies of the field grow. They do not labour or spin. Yet I tell you that not even Solomon in all his splendour was dresst like one of these.

If that is how God clothes the grass of the field, which is here today and tomorrow is thrown into the fire, will he not much more clothe you, O you of little faith? So do not worry, saying, "What shall we eat?" Or "What shall we drink?" or "what shall we wear?" For the pagans run after all these things, and your heavenly Father knows that you need them. But seek first his Kingdom and his righteousness, and all these things will be given to you as well. Therefore do not worry about tomorrow, for tomorrow will worry about itself. Each day has enough trouble of its own.
Matthew 6:25-34.

From this we learn that God is in control, only if we stand in agreement with His word. He will teach us His ways which will sustain us:

Do not wear yourself out to get rich; have the wisdom to show restraint. Cast but a glance at riches, and they are gone, for they will surely sprout wings and fly off to the sky like an eagle. **Proverbs23:4.**

Don't do everything you can just to get rich. Just think about it this way. You work so hard for riches when you are young, then when you get older and can't work; you then spend that money keeping yourself in good health. In the end we pass away and don't get to take anything with us. It just gets given away.

I'm not saying leaving an inheritance for your beloved family is wrong, I am just highlighting the point that becoming rich should not be your primary reason for working hard.
All these worldly possessions will be gone one day.

In order to establish His covenant on the earth.

Parable of the talents; Ruler over much
Matthew 25:21

I am so excited about this entire parable, when I was studying and writing it, it was like God was finally revealing to me what His intentions are for our lives as Christians. If you would really take the time and study this parable as laid out in this book, you will learn the heart of God when it comes to His desires for not only our lives but the entire world and all that dwell within.

This parable is the most important piece of evidence I have come across that God wants you wealthy.

Because this parable is being revealed to us by Jesus himself, we need to understand that there is a very important lesson to be learned.

When the two servants who had doubled what they were given brought the money back to the master, this was the master's response to them;

His master replied, "Well done, good and faithful servant! You have been faithful with a few things; I will put you in charge of many things. Come and share your master's happiness".
Matthew 25:21.

Look at that, the master took back the money, and said to them, well done, I will make you ruler over much. Notice, they didn't receive more money, they received responsibility.

They were both placed in a position of authority because they were found faithful and wise in their use of money which belonged to someone else. They showed their integrity with the little they were entrusted with.

I can't stress this point enough, but here is more proof that it is not about money! It is about your ability, power to rule and not be ruled! Both servants did not receive more money, they were put in a position of power, ruler ship, authority, much more than money can actually buy. Your money; or your use of money is just the training ground, a place of trial which will test your integrity. What type of character you have, are you able to do? Are you a winner or looser?

Your use of money is being monitored by God, to see if you can be found trust worthy, to be put in a position of authority for the Kingdom of God. Today's society, we have become enslaved by money that we are always thinking and wanting more money, but this parable shows clearly that its not about gaining more money, its about being found faithful and obedient with what you have.

So for those of us who keep praying for more money, and "God, I will start giving my tithes when I have more money" then that is the problem right there! That's why you don't have more! You are not being found faithful enough with the little you have so why should God increase you? You are missing out on the master's happiness!

This parable teaches me that being in charge; in a position of command brings happiness. Not just for us, but it will be good for our entire nation, especially those we are in direct contact with.

When the righteous thrive, the people rejoice; when the wicked rule, the people groan.
Proverbs 29:2.

See here again, when the righteous thrive. What does that word "thrive" mean to you? Hungry? Poor? Malnourished? Starving? Frustrated? Can't afford to pay their bills on time? Living below the poverty line? What's your situation?
Are you righteous? Are you settling for just a normal everyday existence?

Thrive, according to the dictionary means; Flourish, to make steady progress; prosper, to do well, be at the high point in ones career, successful. These are powerful words, that when you associate them with this passage, we see that when the righteous obtain all these things, the rest of the world will rejoice. They won't be as much desperation and hunger, all will be taken care of when the righteous are in authority, which is the point, according to the parable of the Talents, God wants us to reach.

Now look at the second part. When the wicked rule, the people groan. If you just turn on your TV or radio today, you will hear a lot of moaning and groaning from all over the world. This upsets me because; this was never Gods intention for the world. What pleasure will He get from creating a world that is in perfect harmony, then filling it with a bunch of money hungry, wicked and decisive people to ruin it for others? Nothing! So the reason there is so much groaning in the world today, is because the righteous are not thriving! The righteous are too busy trying to pay down their debts, keep the roof over their heads and just make it through the month. (I am not talking about all the righteous, please don't be offended.)

But the majority of the righteous are still stumbling forwards in their training, and are still enslaved by money and our needs that we have left these big corporations to be ruled by wicked and evil people, who are only in it for themselves, what they can squeeze out of the poor.

Gods' intention for the world is that the righteous thrive, that you thrive in the little, pass your test and become faithful enough to be in a position of ruler ship, so that the people stop moaning and start giving God all the glory that you are in charge; that you are in authority. We need to take up our positions as ambassadors of Christ. We all have that ability to produce and thrive.

So today begin to prove that you can be faithful with a little, stop focusing on the little you have and start seeking the Kingdom first. Work the job you have to the best of your ability, do whatever you do with all your heart, prove to God that you are faithful with someone else riches so that you can be entrusted with your own.

In order to establish His covenant on the earth.

The world will accept you if you just stay poor.
Blind Bartimaeus
Mark 10:46-52

In the Bible days things were physical, happened in the natural. We would read about wars, read about how God would send a prophet to the nations and discomfort them and send the opposing armies into confusion so they end up fighting themselves. We read about there being no rain, famine, people being sold asunder, and so on. When it was Mainly God Himself doing all of the conquering. But today, it is mostly spiritual; the battlefield has moved from the natural and is now taking place in your mind. The enemy is attacking our emotions and thought processes in order to hinder us from fully reaping the benefits of Gods promises.

So the Bible says, "give and it shall be giving unto you" but the world is saying "buy buy buy, spend spend spend, and you will have. Which is true!

The world is saying "do things our way". While God is saying, "apply your faith, do things my way". So there's a battle going on in your mind.

Who will win?

Let's take a look at this story here. We see a blind man calling out to Jesus for help. Nothing wrong with that, we do it all the time; but here there is a battle going on in his mind because the people around him are telling him not to. He is being discouraged and even told off for disturbing Jesus. He has a decision to make. Listen to them or keep crying out!

Then they came to Jericho. As Jesus and his disciples, together with a large crowd were leaving the city, a blind man, Bartimaeus, was sitting by the road side begging. When he heard that it was Jesus of Nazareth, he began to shout "Jesus, son of David, have mercy on me!" Many rebuked him and told him to be quiet, but he shouted all the more, "Son of David, have mercy on me!" Jesus stopped and said, "Call him." So they called to the blind man, "cheer up! On your feet! He's calling you."

Throwing his cloak aside, he came to his feet and went to Jesus. "What do you want me to do for you?" Jesus asked him. The blind man said, "Rabbi, I want to see."

"Go", Jesus said, "your faith has healed you." Immediately he received his sight and followed Jesus down the road.

Mark 10:46-52.

In this story, this blind man sees a chance, "maybe Jesus can set me free" so he calls out to Jesus by faith. "Jesus, help me."

Notice what the world was saying to him. "Leave Jesus alone," just stay blind basically, just stay in your current situation, don't try anything or do anything different.

Which would you listen to? His situation was desperate, probably like yours, he was fed up of being blind. Are you fed up of your current financial situation? He was being limited from enjoying life by his blindness, are your finances limiting you?

Why not try Jesus? This guy didn't listen to the so called voices of encouragement, his so called friends who where telling him to be quiet. He said "No! Im fed up with my current situation" and he shouts even louder.

You too should try crying out to Jesus if you're fed up like he was.

I need your help in my finances, its limiting me, stopping me from helping others, living my life, Jesus it's depressing me, getting me down and stress out.

Watch, the world is saying "Just stay poor, we will accept you as long as you are complaining like we are". The bank is saying "don't worry, you can count on us". Credit cards are saying "im here for you, just pay me back later, don't worry about it".

Let's see what the Bible recommends about doing things Gods' way.

Do not conform any longer to the pattern of this world, but be transformed by the renewing of your mind. Then you will be able to test and approve what Gods' will is- His good, pleasing and perfect will.

Romans 12:2.

Here the scripture is confirming to us that the battlefield is in the mind. We are encouraged to change the way we think about things, how we evaluate a situation. Don't always do things the way the world encourages.

You have a choice, do things God's way (which is by faith) or listen to the world and just remain the same, doing the same things and getting the same results.

It is a definition of insanity to do the same thing but expect different results.

You need to do something different if you want a different result, change something, your ideas, your motives, your perceptions. The world can relate with you just staying poor, riddled with debt, they understand what you're going through, but they can't accept that you want to give freely and generously to a church.

They don't understand tithes; they don't see the point in offerings to support a church while you are still in debt.

But its working for you, your mind is stable, you're content with what you have, you never go hungry, you're happy, life is good.

So Jesus asks, "What do you want me to do for you?" he says "I want to see", you can put yourself in his place and say, "I need your help with my finances, I struggle to get through the month, its killing me, I need your help"

So Jesus says, "Go, your faith in me and what I can do for you has set you free".

Today, don't worry about what the world thinks; it's just this simple, Jesus said "your faith has set you free" So have faith in the word of God with your finances. Soon it will set you free.

In order to establish His covenant on the earth.

I almost backslid when I saw how the ungodly prosper.
Psalm 73:2-3

One thing we learn from the Bible is that God is unchangeable, but we are changeable. God wants nothing but the best from us, so in order to receive what is rightfully ours according to his promise, we need to do things His way and remain faithful.

So in **psalm 73,** the writer is talking about how it is very easy to backslide from God when we look at the riches of the world. I advise you to study it in your own time to learn how easy it is to remove yourself from the promises of God.

The portion I am focusing on is this:

But as for me, my feet almost slipped; I had almost lost my foothold. For I envied the arrogant. When I saw the prosperity of the wicked.
Psalm 73: 2-3.

In other words, if you are the type of person who spends most of your time watching others, studying and envying how they live outwardly. If you're a person who compares with others your age or younger, you want to keep up with the joneses as it were; then you are heading for disaster.

First of all, the outward display of a person or family might not really be the truth. You have no idea what they did or are doing to have what they have; whether good or evil! You need to take your eyes away.

Believe me, I know this is so hard to do because we see it everywhere, ungodly, sick, wretched, evil people just prospering all over the place. Enjoying worldly wealth so easily while us; good, honest, God fearing people seem to be struggling financially every month.

The world today is doing such a great job of advertising promiscuity, showing sinful acts and advertising them as "you will enjoy yourself if you do these things". We are constantly shown the wealth of openly ungodly people, they advertise them as being happy and contented all the time, we see celebrities in their lifestyle, music artists driving big flash cars, drinking, sleeping around, these modern music videos now getting worse, polluting the minds of our young children; its everywhere. So I understand that you might say it is hard to take your eyes away from it, that its entertainment.
But that is such a feeble excuse for doing something that will only cause you more harm than good. Your foot will slip.

How do we take our eyes off the prosperity of the ungodly?
Well it's very simple; we need to understand things from Gods perspective. What I really love about the Bible is that it doesn't just advise you what not to do, and why, but it also shows you how to do it by giving you the background to the command.

A good man leaves an inheritance for his children's children, but the wealth of the sinner is stored up for the righteous.
Proverbs 13:22.

Wow! This is awesome. I hope you can really understand what this passage is telling us (especially the second part), the wealth of those sinners, ungodly people, basically the world, is being stored up for those of us who will do it right.

In other words, those people who you envy because of their wealth, (if you believe the word of God) their wealth is being stored up for you. It's your wealth! It's your house! Your car! Your big screen TV! Your private Jet! Your millions. Basically what the ungodly are flaunting now, belongs and is promised to you by the word of God. So today I dare you to take your eyes of the worldly, and focus on the word of God, learn to do it his way, change your perspective of things, and view it as they are just looking after your stuff.

I remember when this was first revealed to me; I have a friend who is quite wealthy, his house had big gardens both back and front, which he had to either use a ride-on lawn mower or pay someone else to cut the grass for him. One day we were talking, I mentioned that I had to go home and cut my grass. To which he replied "what grass"? He was basically being sarcastic, making fun of the little bit of grass I had.
Before, this would really offend me, because I had worked hard and long to buy my house, so who was he to make fun of what was mine! But instead of getting offended and angry, the spirit quickly revealed to me that his wealth is being stored up for me, that's my grass when I'm ready to receive it, I will own his grass.

So when he cuts it, he's basically looking after my inheritance. To me now, that was great because he really does a good job of looking after my grass. I'm happy now when I go round there and the lawn is being well looked after, I commend him; I always say "good job, it looks great, the grass is healthy".

So now you see, looking at things from Gods angle will always keep your mind in peace, don't worry about what the world is showing you, when you learn how to do things Gods way, and according to his command, for is glory, you will receive what is promised to you.

In order to establish His covenant on the earth.

Why is the wealth of the ungodly being stored up?

In the last portion, we saw that the wealth of the wicked is being stored up for the righteous (us). But why is that? What is the reasoning behind this storing up? We need it now! We're hungry and desperate now! The world is hurting now! Also if you think about it, it will be for the benefit of the kingdom that we get it now! There are lost, innocent, hurting people out there who we could reach with the gospel if we had the resources now, so what's the hold up?

Well, the hold up is us! Our thinking, our understanding and value of money.

If you don't have the wealth of the wicked or the power of money yet, it is simply because you don't understand how to use it yet, if we had it now, it could potentially do more harm than good. Like a person who wins the lottery after not really working hard for anything, just being lazy and hoping for the best, statistics have shown that those types of people, winning the lottery was the worst thing that ever happened to them. It ruined their life, they were not able to control themselves, they just ran out bought everything they ever wanted, did everything they wanted to do and ended up loosing the true meaning and value of life.

Very devastating.

If you were to receive all the money God desires for you to have today, what would you do with it? Will it just send you into a tail spin? Will it change your character?

So let's understand the Biblical reasoning behind this storing up.

But I will not drive them out in a single year, because the land will become desolate and the wild animals too numerous for you. Little by little I will drive them out before you, until you have increased enough to take possession of the land.
Exodus 23:29-30.

You see, God does things in order; He has a step by step growing process He takes all his beloved through. In this portion of scripture, we see that the Israelites were promised by God the land, but they didn't get it all straight away. They weren't in possession of it all yet, simply because they were unable to take care of it, the work would have been too much for them, it would have overwhelmed them, so they had to be patient and grow enough in order to look after what God had promised them.
So here is the principle; as we have learnt already, God never changes, His ways remain the same; the principles are steadfast in all aspects and generations. What we are doing in this book is to study these Biblical principles and apply them to our finances to see if we can reproduce the same kingdom results in order to prove that God wants us wealthy.

So it is with the wealth God has promised us, we can't have it all at once.

It will be too much for us to handle and use effectively. What would you do with it? We might develop a selfish mentality and forget where it came from, or why we have it, and then we run out with it and have a train wreck because it was too much too soon. God wouldn't want that for us! According to this principle, He will release it gradually to those who are willing and are capable of growing with it.

It is your promise as a child of God to be wealthy according to **Deuteronomy 8:18**. It is already promised to you. If you are not yet living in Gods abundant provision, it is simply because you are not ready for it yet, you have to grow and develop your thinking, trust that it comes from God not just for your benefit and to serve your agenda, but its for the use of developing the Kingdom of God.
You have to start by learning to rely and obey God with the little you have now before you can grow.

"But God when I start making more money, I will start tithing and giving to support your church"
That mentality will cause you to miss out on the training process. So you want God to start working for you before you obey His command?

Bring the whole tithes into the storehouse, that they might be food in my house. Test me in this, says the Lord almighty "and see if I will not open the flood gates of heaven and pour you out such a blessing that you will not have enough room for it".
Malachi 3:10.

God will always be the initiator of the giving process; He has already sent his son Jesus Christ to die for our sins.

What more do we want? To prove Himself to who? To impress who? Show up for what?

We are trying to negotiate and bring an Almighty God down to our level, while He's trying to bring you up to His level. He's God!

Then we say "but God if I just win the lottery, I will build a church",
Guess what? He's built it already without your help.

We need to grow gradually in order to be able to receive the prosperity which according to the Bible (which is the word of God) is our inheritance.
So when we see a land flowing with milk and honey, the word flowing, in the English dictionary means, "to keep moving, in motion, run, circulating, move constantly and steadily, increasing".

Gods' blessings flow. So today ask yourself, where is your money flowing to?
If Gods' provision flows into your house then remains there, it will not continue flowing or increase in abundance. But if it can flow through you, if you are found trust worthy to being a source of the flow into the lives of others and the church, then God can begin increasing the flow as you are able to distribute it wisely.

If God can get money through you, He will get it to you. As long as you can handle it, the increase will begin.

In order to establish His covenant on the earth.

Gods' Storehouse
Malachi 3:10

"Bring the whole tithe into the storehouse, that there may be food in my house. Test me in this," *says the Lord Almighty, "and see if I will not throw open the floodgates of heaven and pour out so much blessing that you will not have room enough for it."*
Malachi 3:10.

This portion of scripture is so important, and is the clearest and most direct passage, which confirms the need and benefits associated with tithes and offerings.

First of all, allow me to put the entire book of Malachi into context. This is the last book of the Old Testament (Before Jesus comes on the scene). The entire nation of Israel (who are Gods chosen people) have been so rebellious, God has lifted his hand of protection from them and they are torn apart by wars, dispensation, plagues and so on and so forth. So God sends a prophet (Malachi) to call his people back to order. To re-align them up with whom they are, in order to reap the benefits of His will for the entire nation of Israel.

One of the first things God sets back up is the principles of giving. He re-establishes the laws and commands; He reminds them of the importance of giving according to His command. He confirms the order, and uses the word storehouse.

I urge you to study the entire book of Malachi when you can; it will confirm so many things I'm trying to get across to you in this book.

Now the word storehouse means; a depository, store, depot, warehouse, place of distribution. So what God is saying here is, bring your whole tithes into my place of distribution. Why? So that I may have the ability to distribute it to those who are needy; so that the Gospel may be preached from a specific place. Gods' storehouse is the place where you are being fed the word. Whether it is your local church, Television ministry or a pastoral / spiritual father. From wherever source the true word of God is being taught to you and others.

The reason this order has been set up in this way, is so that the work of the ministry will be financed by your giving; and the needy will have a place to go for support. If a church is struggling financially, they can't effectively operate and share the word on a consistent basis! They can't provide a useful service; or help the poor!
So God establishes His law; and sets in it, that anyone who will fulfil the requirements will receive such a blessing, that they won't have enough room to keep it; which replenishes His storehouse; in order that those who are in need have a place they can receive from. So according to the word of God, let's see how this storehouse or place of distribution was filled; It is done by people giving offerings freely to the church. Your gift to a ministry is deposited for distribution in times of need. But the most important ones are the tithes; for which, there are three main ones:

1: **First fruits**, which is found in these passages:

Leviticus 27:30-33. Nehemiah 10:37. Numbers 18:24-32.

This tithe is ten percent of your income. The first fruits mean; the first of what ever you have managed to bring into your home.

Whether it is through Government help, working or being in business. Whatever your pay is. This is referred to as the Lords portion. In other words, it belongs to God! It is Holy and belongs to Him, to do with however He pleases; it doesn't belong to you.
Now if you don't want to hear this and you're thinking "but it's my money, I worked hard for it, I need it!" then please, keep your money! But if you can acknowledge that this law has been set by God Him self, and that it belongs to Him, then you need to be giving it according to His word, with a cheerful heart. It has got to be the best! The first thing you think of or even do with whatever income you receive. You should put it aside as the Lords, and it is before you pay your bills. So basically you don't tithe on what is leftover, you tithe on what comes in! Then pay your bills with the leftovers. Don't give God leftover, it wont help you in the long run.

2: **Business Tithe**, Which is found in these passages:

Deuteronomy 14:22-27; Deuteronomy 12:5-7.

This tithe is for those who are in business. If you own your own business, or as the Bible puts it, your own land. You bring ten percent of what your business has made over the year. This will be brought at the time of the feast, so you could say like an end of year party, where you would eat and celebrate what God has increased you.

The way this would work is that all the people in the church who own businesses, would store up the ten percent from the year, and fund a celebration in the church, to give thanks to God for how He has blessed the businesses. So you need to understand that this celebration can only be done if your business has turned over a profit in the year.

This basically means that it is up to Gods' provision and favour on your business that would determine the scale of the celebration or even making the celebration happen. If your business makes a loss, it can't tithe ten percent of nothing! So what God would do, is He would bless the businesses that tithe so that there would be a celebration at the end of the year. If there was no increase in that year, there would be no celebration, simple; you can't celebrate with what you don't have! So the bigger the increase of your business in the year, the bigger the celebration would be. Wouldn't you like that for your business? To be able to celebrate and give thanks to God for how He has favoured your business through the year.

3: **Tithe for the needy and workers in the church** (every third year) which are found in these passages:

Deuteronomy 14:28. Deuteronomy 26:12.

This third tithe is taken at the end of every third year. The tithes from that year would be stored up, and then at the end of the year, it should be distributed to the workers and the needy in the church, the widows, orphans, elderly, un-employed, disabled, volunteers, leaders, staff, and so on. This is how God would support these people. It is the distribution of tithes from the entire third year that supported these groups of people. They were or are supposed to be taken care of by the Church.

Now there is some confusion as to whether you tithe on your entire income from your employment, because you get your money after your national insurance has been paid, and your income tax has been taken out by the government. So some people ask the question "do we tithe on the gross income (which is before tax)? Or on the net income (which is after tax)?

This is a justified question and the answer is this; in the Bible days, the church used the tithes to establish schools, hospitals, roads, economies etc. So the tithes were used to fund these services as the church was basically the government. But now, we have governing bodies which provide these services, they are being funded by the tax which is taken out of our income, so that sector of things have already been taken care of by them, so you don't need to tithe on your entire gross income because the need for schools, hospitals, roads, services and so on are already taken care of by the tax we pay. So saying that your tithe should be ten percent of your net income, what you get after tax is correct just on the basis that the modern churches do not provide those services anymore, the government do.

Another point that people ask me is; "then does this mean we should be tithing three times?"
Well let's try to answer that as well. What have we learnt so far about Gods' store house? It is a place of distribution; how does this place of distribution get filled? By the tithes of the people (you and I). What are tithe? They are ten percent of income. The income comes from God. So the store house is only filled if God holds up His end of the bargain, to bless and increase us so that we may fund the needs associated with the spreading of the Gospel.

I know some people then get scared and say "I can't give away that much!" Well maybe that's why you don't have that much, could that thinking be what is hindering Gods' abundance! You need to get rid of that scared, greedy, selfish, me first mentality, and be found faithful and obedient with the little you have, so that God can begin to see you as a vessel He can use to reach a hurting world.

In the days where these tithes are found, there was such a spirit of giving because they were so blessed, they lived in such a level of abundance that we can only dream of. They relied so much on Gods' provision that they could tithe three times without going hungry.

That's even before the seven offerings. Can you imagine how much abundance they must have had in order to tithe three times and give seven offerings as well?

This is what God wants for every one of us, to be living in such abundance that we recognise giving as a blessing, we give so freely with a grateful heart because we recognise and have proved that our help comes from the Lord.

We need to be wealthy, business owners, entrepreneurs, philanthropists, generous in order for Gods' store house to be filled. We can only tithe on what we have, so God would increase what we have, in order to fill His place of distribution.

One other thing to note here is that what happened in the natural in the Old Testament has now, (through Jesus Christ) been implanted into the hearts as New Testament believers. So it is now more of a heart condition and motives, that God receives our gifts and offerings. Before He can increase us, He looks at our heart, and then increases those who are faithful and obedient in order that there is enough provision in His storehouse to keep supporting all those involved in the ministry and also in spreading the Gospel of Jesus Christ.

You give what you want to, what you feel comfortable giving, and let God be the judge of whether you are capable of being entrusted with such abundance.

We haven't seen riches until God shows up with it.

Conclusion

I pray sincerely; that in the name of Jesus, the words you have read in this book shall be planted in your heart and in time, according to the will of God, produce a harvest for others to see and benefit from.

That you won't just prove this understanding, but you will share it with others, believers and un-believers alike. I pray that as you have studied this book, you will truly apply yourself to it and that your understanding be opened up to the various truths highlighted in it, your character be transformed and you be found faithful, trust worthy enough, not only to receive Christ's abundance in your life, but be faithful enough to use it according to the word of God.

May you become a channel through which others are blessed.

Beloved, I wish above all things that thou mayest prosper and be in health even as thy soul prospereth.
3John 1:2(KJV)

Be blessed in the name of Jesus, as you prove that God wants you wealthy for the purpose of spreading the gospel to a dying world.

Amen

Acknowledgements

Let me take the time to acknowledge a few of the people in my life whose support made this entire book possible.

A great thanks to my pastor, Mick Shah, Anna his wife and their wonderful son Ethan (Who is also my God son)

My Mother Julie Croydon. Who has been my role model and an inspiration in all areas of my life.

My Dad Ven Isaac Tejevbo. Who actually introduced me to the Christian life, and has encouraged and championed me in my walk with God ever since.

Charlene Logan. Who is the greatest graphics designer I have ever come across. She designed the cover of this book, and has been a great support and motivator throughout this project.

The entire congregation of The Revival Church Basingstoke. Who have been forced to listen to me teaching on the points highlighted in this book for the past three years, and proved them to be true and absolutely effective.

My darling wife Kerry-Ann Tejevo, who has been nagging me for so long to better myself while not actually realising that it is only the spirit working through me that makes me a better person.

A great appreciation to my close friends Sammy and Cecilia Njenga. Who kindly opened their house to me so I could get away and truly focus on finishing this project.

I dedicate this Book to the apple of my eye, my heartbeat, my beloved son. Josiah Keve Tejevo. I do it all for your future son.
I love you.

All I do is for the glory of God my father. All praise Honour and Adoration to His mighty name.
This is just another tool in the masters' hand.

For speaking engagements you can reach me either via my website or by email.
www.tejgroup.org
www.u-can2.net.
E mail: btejevo@tejgroup.org

Be Blessed.

<u>Notes</u>

Notes

<u>Notes</u>

<u>Notes</u>

<u>Notes</u>